HISTORIC TAVERNS *and Tea Rooms* OF MAINE

Kathy Kenny & Bill Kenny

THE History PRESS

Published by The History Press
Charleston, SC
www.historypress.com

First published 2021

Manufactured in the United States

ISBN 9781467148986

Library of Congress Control Number: 2021934082

Notice: The information in this book is true and complete to the best of our knowledge. It is offered without guarantee on the part of the author or The History Press. The author and The History Press disclaim all liability in connection with the use of this book.

For Maddie, who loves tea parties; and Kimberly and Tim, who own a lovely tea set; and the Ladies Literary Lunch Book Group, tea drinkers all!

And to the members of the Cumberland Curmudgeon Club, who meet weekly at the modern-day tavern Rachel's on the Green, located at the Val Halla Golf Course in Cumberland, Maine, to hear, discuss and solve all of the local, state and national problems of the day while doing their part to keep the tradition of early Maine taverns alive and well.

CONTENTS

ACKNOWLEDGEMENTS

This book is the result of our desire to share a particular part of Maine's history with you and the great amount of research and information collected by a number of people and organizations. We greatly appreciate all of the support they provided. Any omission of acknowledgement to any person who contributed material is unintentional. Whenever we mentioned the title of the book as *Historic Taverns and Tea Rooms of Maine*, people were overwhelmingly excited about the subject and very eager to provide information, photos and personal stories to aid in our research. We thank you all!

Historical societies are worth their weight in gold! As a resource for historical matters, they are the best. Their friendly staff, their knowledge, their photos, their care of artifacts and their pleasure in preserving and sharing items entrusted to them all add up to a wonderful treasure for our citizens, our towns and our state. These historical societies are mostly run by donations and rely largely on volunteers who provide the tours, the programs, the maintenance of the collections, the exhibits and the research for all of us to enjoy. Those of us who realize the worth of these societies must see that they are not forgotten by donating or volunteering our time to help preserve our history.

We want to express our gratitude and thanks to the following historical societies and the tireless help their researchers gave:

Sofia Yolouris at the Maine Historical Society was a great help in finding images of Maine's taverns and tea rooms. Thanks so much!

Bryce Waldrop and his staff—Hope Shelley, Lorraine Morse and Bill Farr—at the Historical Society of Wells and Ogunquit provided us with much information and photos from that area. We thank you all for your assistance!

Carolyn Small, a real treasure-trove of information and the curator of the Cumberland Historical Society, helped us once again by providing us with photos, postcards and information on taverns and tea rooms in Cumberland. She also referred us to contacts in Turner for information on a tea room that was located there. Thanks again, Carolyn.

Katie Worthing of the Yarmouth Historical Society provided abundant information on Yarmouth's taverns and tea rooms. This is the second book that she has helped provide research information for us. Her continued support and in-depth knowledge are always greatly appreciated. Cheers, Katie!

Paige Lilly at the Castine Historical Society stepped up as well, finding very interesting information about that town's taverns and tea rooms. We appreciate your assistance.

Surry Historical Society's John Curtis helped us a great deal in our research, as did Willie Granston of Great Harbor Maritime Museum in Northeast Harbor. Thanks to you both.

William Chapman at the Bethel Historical Society did a lot of research and provided us not only with information about that town's taverns and tea rooms but also connected us with his mother, Amy Wight Chapman, granddaughter of one of the original owners of Farwell and Wight's Tea Room. She provided us with wonderful information and an actual photo of the inside of the tea room for use in this book. We are so glad you shared your information with us!

Lydia Brown at the North Haven Historical Society, Bonnie Healy at the Lubec Historical Society and Kristen Camp at the Kennebec Historical Society also did research for us, as did others at the Norway Historical Society. Our thanks to you all.

Certain individuals also gave us both encouragement and information that helped greatly in collecting the necessary facts for the book. A big thank-you to Pam Whitehead, Sara Sullivan, Kimberly Kenny and Cheryl and Spencer Collin. Thanks also to Rosemary and Peter Goranites for their diligence in researching for us. Ron and Barbara Beedy deserve our heartful thanks for sharing an abundance of information about the family's Silver Bell Tea Room. They also introduced us to Heather Nadeau of Turner, the great-great-granddaughter of the Silver Bell's original owners. She has rescued the original tea room and gave us a lovely tour of the building. Thank you all for a very resourceful and enjoyable day!

We also want to extend a large thank-you to our neighbor photographer, Peter Goranites, of Cumberland for the great authors photo and to our editor, Mike Kinsella of The History Press, for all his help and suggestions.

Lastly, a special thanks to an unknown Kittery police officer. We stopped at the station to get directions, and he went above and beyond in not only giving us directions to nearby Eliot but also figuring out where the specific taverns we were looking for were located and how to find them. Thanks to one of Kittery's finest!

PREFACE

The story of Maine's early taverns is an account of an all-but-forgotten way of life. Although most have disappeared because of progress, many have survived in unexpected places, from the middle of cities through the suburbs and into the countryside. The men (and women!) who ran the taverns reflect the backbone of Maine's character, and the existing buildings themselves are tangible proof of our state's resilience and history. The many interesting stories of some of these taverns are told in the following pages of this book. The variety of each of these taverns presents an overview of community, commerce and politics during Maine's growth as a state. They represent the forgotten traces of the past, the courage and strength it took to clear a piece of land, build a house and start a tavern.

A lot of these taverns have now disappeared, a few are still in existence as taverns or businesses and still others have been converted to private homes or museums. The taverns presented here are only a sampling of the historic taverns of Maine; the list is not intended to be a comprehensive one or descriptions of all those that were in operation during Maine's early history. Reading about these early taverns will enforce the necessity of understanding our history and the need to preserve it.

—*Bill*

In the following pages, you will discover the interesting social history of tea and tea rooms. Each photo and description offers a fascinating view into the world of early Maine tea rooms that helped establish tea as a national drink. Although this is not a complete list of Maine tea rooms, it is nevertheless an interesting representation. As a part of the tea movement, these tea rooms brought great pleasure to all who frequented them and contributed greatly to a unique part of Maine's history.

When some of today's women were asked the question, "What are your thoughts when you hear the words 'tea room'?" their answers were surprisingly similar:

- Rosemary G.: "My thoughts are of taking your time, enjoying a cup of tea and having conversations. Eating at the Puritan Tea Room in Portland with my mom."
- Elaine S.: "I think of fancy cups and saucers, teapots and vases of flowers. Tea carts with the specialty foods of the day. Ladies wearing hats and gloves."
- Kim K.: "When I think of tea rooms I always think of 'high tea.' Lace tablecloths, floral-patterned bone china teapots with matching cups and saucers and espergnes filled with pastries and small, savory sandwiches."
- Pam W.: "Warm and enchanting atmosphere. Ladies wearing white gloves and hats. Sampling both sweet and savory treats along with tea from bone china teapots."
- Diane B.: "I love bone china and am impressed with the variety of teacups and saucers, small plates and teapots used in tea rooms. I enjoy the many choices of teas and finger foods offered and the gift items for sale."
- Pat W.: "I consider them to be very feminine-feeling places. Pleasant places that don't urge you to rush through your meal. Soft music and quiet conversations."

I find it astonishing that the perception of tea rooms has not changed over the years and that today's women hold the same thoughts as did their ancestors over 130 years ago. Such definite, strong feelings and visuals indicate that tea rooms still hold a special place in today's society and that they have certainly stood the test of time.

If you have never visited a tea room before, then please try to do so. Pleasure, peace and delicious food await you!

—*Kathy*

INTRODUCTION

Taverns and tea rooms played significant roles throughout Maine's history. The taverns were originally established in the 1700s to provide rest stops for stagecoaches and horses and to provide refreshments and lodging for travelers. Tea rooms became popular in the late 1800s and early 1900s during the great tea movement. They offered women a place to congregate socially and hold meetings without the socially required male escorts.

Maine women became the owners, managers and workers in the tea rooms that were established as a result of the tea movement of the early 1900s. This was significant because it was the first time that women were able to become an integral part of the business world that, until this time, had been dominated by men. Tea rooms gave women the unprecedented gift of business and financial independence.

Both taverns and tea rooms maintained a great influence on the community, the culture and the commerce of Maine life. Both offered meeting places and refreshments to those involved in the various events of the day, which often included business meetings, social events, educational forums, temperance meetings, suffragette meetings, cultural entertainment and political meetings. Taverns run by Maine men and some Maine women were also used to conduct town and government business and hold trials for circuit judges and were the venue to form new militias.

BURNHAM TAVERN, MACHIAS (1770–PRESENT)

The Burnham Tavern is of significance not only in the history of Maine but also in American history. It was built in 1770.

In early June 1775, the men and women in the settlement of Machias faced a very difficult dilemma. Hearing of the news from Lexington and Concord, they were faced with an ultimatum. In order to get their critical supplies—such as flour, rice, sauerkraut, vinegar, grains, vegetables and porter (beer) and, more importantly, horses and powder for their muskets—the settlers had to continue to ship lumber to Boston to build barracks for British troops. If they refused, they faced the wrath of Lieutenant James Moore, commander of the armed British vessel *Margaretta*, which was anchored in the harbor with guns leveled at their homes. Less than 10 percent of the powder needed in the colonies was produced in the colonies; the rest had to be imported, as did most of the grains and vegetables. The production of farm products in the colonies was insufficient at that time in our history; more than 80 percent had to be imported. Horses came from England and other European ports as well. If they complied with Lieutenant Moore's orders, the colonists would be betraying the American cause, which was to avoid buying supplies from England. Lieutenant Moore's and other English ships would simply blockade needed goods if the colonies didn't fall in line.

Vigorous debate took place in the taproom of Job Burnham's Tavern as the settlers struggled with what to do. Jeremiah O'Brien, Job Burnham's brother-in-law, was among those who argued for aggressive action. O'Brien argued hard for the citizens to capture the British commander and the *Margaretta.* Jeremiah's arguments prevailed, and with the support of his five brothers and several veterans of the French and Indian Wars, plans were made to take Lieutenant Moore while he sat in church on June 12, 1775. Things did not go exactly as planned, however. Lieutenant Moore chose a seat in the church where he could view the footbridge just above Bad Little Falls, and he spotted men crossing with scythes and pitchforks along with a few muskets. He immediately surmised that the crop the settlers were about to harvest was himself along with his men also attending church services. Moore escaped through a church window, and with the element of surprise on his side, he managed to make it back to his ship. As soon as he boarded the *Margaretta*, he ordered the ship to set sail, and it began moving down the river to the open waters of the Atlantic. Some one hundred Patriots, still armed primarily with farm implements, followed in two merchant ships, the *Falmouth Packet* and the *Unity.* In the battle that ensued, Lieutenant Moore

Burnham Tavern. *Collections of Maine Historical Society. From* Life of Captain Jeremiah O'Brien, Machias, Maine *(Andrew M. Sherman, Morristown, NJ: Sherman, 1902), MHS 31168.*

was shot and the *Margaretta* captured. Burnham Tavern was immediately converted into a hospital, as both sides had suffered casualties. Lieutenant Moore succumbed to his wounds, and there is a chest in Burnham Tavern today that is said to be stained with his blood.

Jeremiah O'Brien went on to serve the new country as a privateer, and early in these endeavors, he was captured and imprisoned in England, but he escaped and returned to fight again. Burnham Tavern, now a museum, has many mementos of the O'Brien family, some personal and others relating to several ships named after them.

From its gambrel roof to its millstone steps the tavern is a great example of the design of buildings of that time in American history. The tavern is furnished much as it was in the 1770s, and many of those furnishings have very interesting histories, giving visitors an idea of the lifestyle of early Maine settlers.

In recognition of the Burnham Tavern's importance, it has been designated as a National Historic Site by the U.S. Department of the Interior, and in 1974, the tavern was selected as one of the twenty-one homes in the United States with the most significance to the American Revolution, the only one so designated in what is now the state of Maine. The Hannah Weston Chapter of the Daughters of the American Revolution now runs the tavern as a museum.

MAINE'S TAVERNS AND TEA rooms have a special and unique history that includes such notables as John Adams while traveling as a circuit judge; suffragette Susan B. Anthony, Edna Thomas, great-granddaughter of Seth Thomas, originator of the Seth Thomas Clock Company; Isabel Greenwood, wife of Chester Greenwood of earmuff fame; Maine's first governor, William King; Benjamin Franklin; and the Marquis de Lafayette. Maine tea rooms even had the patronage of First Lady Eleanor Roosevelt. The planning of the first naval battle of the Revolutionary War and the signing of the final papers giving Maine its independence from Massachusetts were signed in Maine taverns.

These taverns and tea rooms were at the forefront of many of Maine's social, economic and political events and, even today, are remembered as an essential part of Maine's history.

EARLY TRAVEL IN MAINE

Before Maine became a separate state on March 15, 1820, it was part of Massachusetts called the District of Maine. Travel in the early days was rudimentary; there weren't any established roads at that time. The early settlers located their homes along the rivers and the Atlantic Ocean to be close to water transportation. Much of the travel was by water, and those going inland either walked, rode horseback or took carriages when the rutted trails were passable. In the winter months those walking used snowshoes and carried poles with large wooden disks on the bottom for balance and support. These were much like modern-day ski poles. The first transportation network in the territory that became the state of Maine was composed of waterways—streams, rivers, ponds, lakes and the long tidal estuaries and bays along the deeply indented coast. By using the waterways and carrying their canoes and small boats over land that separated bodies of water, the Red Paint people, the later Indian, the explorer, the pioneer and eventually the white settler were able to travel throughout the state. With a ready-made system of transportation all around them, early Mainers were not about to spend their energy building roads they did not need. They followed the Indian trails along the banks of rivers and streams, making them a little wider and a little deeper. The settlers felled timber and cleared a rough road through the forest to early shipyards. Moreover, they had enough to do around their local area without yearning to visit the next settlement. Likely as not, the next settlement was just up or down the river, so they traveled by boat.

There were no legally established roads between towns and settlements in the early 1600s, and when the first roads came along, they were built close to the shorelines of the ocean, rivers and streams. The District of Maine could not boast of its first made road, the Kennebec Road by the Sea, until 1653, when the crown commissioners of Massachusetts came to the district to hold court and complained of the lack of decent roads. The Kennebec Road by the Sea was a crude road running from Kittery through York, Wells, Saco and Scarborough. These settlements were ordered to make "straight and convenient pathways along the east coast for man and horse." The road was extended north to Falmouth, now Portland, a few years later. To say these roads were crude would be an understatement; these were basically two rows of cart wheel ruts with a horse path in the middle. This constituted what would become known as the Kings Highway right up to just prior to the American Revolution in the mid-eighteenth century. The colonists referred to them as "trodden paths." They were rocky, poorly drained and breached by unpredictable streams along the way. In summer months, the roads were paths of choking dust, and when the first rains came, the unfortunate traveler sunk to his knees in the mud. John Adams, who was to become the second president of the United States, rode horseback over this road to attend the king's court at Pownalborough, now named Wiscasset, to attend to his duties as a riding circuit lawyer in the king's court of law for all of the District of Maine, which, at that time, was still under the rule of King George III.

One of the great contributions the colonials made to America's road system was the milestone. These stone markers were placed to help travelers determine the distance to their destinations. Benjamin Franklin's name is often evoked in relation to these mile markers because of his role as joint deputy postmaster under colonial rule and as the first U.S. postmaster general. Franklin is credited with devising a system of charging for postage based on mileage, which may have prompted the placement of markers to measure each mile along major roads. Various towns placed these markers to aid travelers in navigating and planning for overnight stays along their routes. Markers, some made of wood and others made of stone, were usually carved with one or more letters and numbers, indicating the distance from other cities. Markers along the King's Highway in Maine were usually carved with a *B* and a number indicating the distance from that point to Boston.

Some accounts state that Benjamin Franklin rode along the King's Highway with his invention, the odometer, attached to a wheel of a wagon and that he placed a wooden marker at every mile. Other wagons were said

Mile marker B136, Cumberland. *Author photo.*

Mile marker 136 plaque, Cumberland. *Author photo.*

to follow him, replacing his wooden markers with the carved stone markers, some of which survive today.

Because the population and settlements were increasing, more mail delivery was occurring and there was a need to get mail from the colonies to the District of Maine. The need for getting mail delivered was the impetus to build passable roads to replace the rough trails.

THE JED PROUTY TAVERN AND INN, BUCKSPORT (1820–PRESENT)

The Jed Prouty Tavern and Inn, located at 57 Main Street, was built by Asa Peabody in 1783 as a two-family home.

In 1820, the building was purchased by a man named Sparhawk and converted to a tavern and inn. This tavern was on a major stagecoach route between Bangor and Castine. The name "Jed Prouty" is based on a play written by Richard Golden (1854–1909), an American stage actor and comedian whose most famous role was Old Jed Prouty in a play of the same name. Golden helped create and nationalize the genre of "Downeast humor," which made him one of the celebrated comedians of

Jed Prouty Tavern. *Collections of Bucksport Historical Society, MHS 14461.*

his generation. *Old Jed Prouty* was about a comedic Maine Yankee tavern keeper living in the coastal town of Bucksport. Golden's wife, Dora Wiley, was born in Bucksport, not far from Golden's own hometown of Bangor.

Many prominent people stayed at the Jed Prouty Tavern, including Daniel Webster, Martin Van Buren, William Henry Harrison, Jefferson Davis, Andrew Jackson and John Tyler.

The tavern closed in the mid-1990s and was converted to senior citizen housing. The building was listed in the National Register of Historic Places in 1986.

The Black Horse Tavern, Belfast (1705–Present)

The Black Horse Tavern is a historic tavern on Searsport Avenue (U.S. Route 1) in Belfast built in 1795 and was the city's first tavern located on the eastern side of the Passagassawakeag River. The house was built about 1795 by Jerome Stephenson, a veteran of the American Revolutionary War who moved to Belfast in 1784. Stephenson was prominent in local civic affairs, serving as a selectman in 1785. Although he built the house for his family, he converted it into a tavern in 1800, a role it fulfilled under his son and grandson, until about 1852. The sign used to identify the tavern is now stored in the house. The building, now a private residence, was added to the National Register of Historic Places in 1982.

Mail did not begin in the District of Maine until 1673. In the early days, mail was delivered by post riders, a delivery system that provided somewhat irregular scheduled delivery. Routes were predefined, and there were distance markers and waypoints along the way.

These post riders collected and delivered mail over their route, meeting up with other riders at scheduled times and at scheduled places to exchange forwarded items. Correspondence and even small parcels, such as liquor bottles, could be exchanged until they reached their final destination at a reasonable cost. The riders carried the mail in the four pockets of their mochila, a saddle pouch much like a knapsack or haversack that fit snugly over the saddle and was quickly switched from one horse to another. Letters were wrapped in oil silk to protect them from moisture. By using this method, correspondence could pass reliably from rider to rider and cover a considerable distance in a reasonable time at a reduced cost. Each rider rode about six to eight miles in a day, so it took about ten to twelve days for a piece of mail to travel just one hundred miles.

Hall's Tavern, Falmouth (1800–Present)

Hall's Tavern, also once known as the Falmouth Tavern, and now the Quaker Tavern B&B and Inn, is a historic tavern at 377 Gray Road (Route 100) in Falmouth. It was built about 1800 as a private home and served for many years in the nineteenth century as a traveler accommodation. It is one of Falmouth's few surviving buildings of the period.

The house was built by Nicholas Hall, a farmer originally from Dover, New Hampshire. The house was in the Hall extended family for most

Hall's Tavern, Falmouth. *Author photo.*

of the nineteenth century and was probably converted into a tavern by Nicholas Hall's son Ozni, who acquired the property in 1823. The house was moved circa 1826–27, when the present Gray Road alignment was made, which may also be when it was made into a tavern. The interior of the house retains impressive Federal period woodwork and finishes. The tavern taproom, to the right of the entrance, retains original plaster walls with stencil work stylistically similar to that of the early eighteenth-century itinerant artist Moses Eaton. It was listed in the National Register of Historic Places in 1978.

WHEN WE TALK ABOUT "reasonable cost," it would not seem reasonable at today's costs to mail a letter. It cost about a day's pay to send a single letter in the mid-1700s. Moreover, it was the person receiving the letter or parcel who had to pay, not the sender. There weren't any regular mail deliveries. The post riders prior to that time waited until they had enough letters to pay the expenses of the trip. It was not unusual for weeks to pass before enough mail was collected to make the trip worthwhile. These post riders also carried articles for people along their route and did all sorts of errands along their way. They distributed the news when there were not any newspapers, paid and collected bills, promoted taverns and inns along their routes, served as guides to travelers and became trusted and liked, as they were thought of as the connection to the outside world by the early citizens of the District of Maine. The government did not mind that post riders did these things as long as they did not interfere with the carrying of the mail. The roads of that time, however, were little more than widened bridle paths, making travel slow, uncertain and uncomfortable, especially during winter months and the spring muddy season. The taverns and inns along the way offered a place to rest and obtain food and drink and became the meeting places where people could hear about the news from the outside world and drop off and collect their mail and parcels being delivered by these post riders.

The tavern also served as a post office. Originally, the practice was to put your posts on a table, and travelers would then take them along the route with them. It was commonly accepted that the travelers had the right to read your mail, providing a bit of entertainment for them along the way. Later on, mail arrived in the communities the same way that it left, by post riders, eventually becoming more organized and efficient. Mail delivery was improved with the creation of the Boston Post Road, along which post riders carried letters and guided travelers. Shortly after declaring independence, the Continental Congress established the Postal Service to improve the efficiency and effectiveness of mail delivery, which prior to this time was erratic and not regulated. Benjamin Franklin was named the first postmaster general and implemented the needed changes.

The Lindsey Tavern, Wells (1800–Present)

The Lindsey Tavern in Wells was built by Matthew Lindsey, a native of York, in 1799. It opened to the public as a tavern in 1800. The tavern served as the post office for thirty-seven years, with Matthew Lindsey as the postmaster. According to the Town of Wells Town Report in 1847, soldiers returning from the War of 1812 were entertained there. It is reported that "some of the soldiers lay on the kitchen floor while those who were preparing the food stepped over them." The Lindsey Tavern hosted many noteworthy guests. The most prominent was the Marquis de Lafayette, who came to Maine on June 24, 1825, by way of South Berwick after having spent the night in Dover, New Hampshire. As Lafayette entered the town of Wells, he was received by Horace Porter, chief marshal of the day, and a throng of citizens. He was escorted to the Lindsey Tavern, where he ate dinner and

Lindsey Tavern, Wells. *Author photo.*

delivered an address to the townspeople. The chaise, a two-wheeled carriage for one or two persons with a folding top, on which he rode into town was featured when Wells celebrated its 250th anniversary in 1903.

In an article by Nancy McCallum, community news editor, in the *York County Coast Star* newspaper in 1980, it was reported that "stepping into the Lindsey Tavern is like taking a history lesson, circa 1799, when the tavern was built." She goes on to say that even in 1980, large murals and artwork from the early days of the tavern were still on display. "At first glance, the front hallway looks like an old post office, with a coat rack on one wall holding a powder horn, cutlass, canteen, and ammunition satchel, as well as an overcoat and a coonskin cap." As of 1980, the original floors that the soldiers returning from the War of 1812 walked on still remained in the tavern. The tavern is now home of the Feiles Restaurant Irish Pub at 1619 Post Road in Wells.

BARNARD'S TAVERN, KENNEBUNK (1830–PRESENT)

Located in Kennebunk, Barnard's Tavern is one of the town's oldest houses with a diverse and rich history of its own. The picturesque Maine town is home to several other historic buildings, including many shipbuilders' homes. The main building of the tavern was built prior to the American Revolution, with the connecting ell and barn dating to sometime around 1830–40. The tavern was named after its original owner, Joseph Barnard, who operated a hostelry (lodging) until his death in 1817. Barnard drove the first mail and passenger coach from Portsmouth to Portland in 1787 and went on to become Kennebunk's second postmaster.

Barnard's Tavern, Kennebunkport. *Author photo.*

His wife continued to run the tavern after his death until it was sold in 1823 to Timothy Frost, who ran the tavern until 1853. The next family to occupy the property was the Curtises, who managed a farm during the Civil War. It later became a rooming house and, in the twentieth century, an orphanage for fourteen to twenty children. The historic tavern has seen its share of distinguished guests, including the Marquis de Lafayette in 1825.

As the house was restored over the years, several architectural fragments and accessories were unearthed from other buildings in the area. The clock tower, designed by Kennebunk architect William Barry, was originally part of the Wells Town Hall and is now all that remains of the old town hall building. The red raised panel door came from Hammond Farm in North Berwick, and the windmill, another relic of North Berwick, came from Perkins Farm and dates to 1902.

THE LEIGHTON TAVERN, CUMBERLAND (1800–PRESENT)

The Leighton Tavern was built about 1800 on the Gray Road (Route 100) by Andrew Leighton. The tavern was strategically situated along the old stagecoach route from Falmouth, now Portland, to Bakertown, now Lewiston. It is the oldest and one of the best known of the old Cumberland taverns.

At the time the Leighton Tavern was in existence, travelers and teamsters leading ox-driven wagons were traveling along this route, and this tavern was a favorite place for the travelers and teamsters to stop, rest and get their horses and oxen refreshed as well. The Leightons had seven sons and one daughter. Two of Andrew's sons served aboard the privateer vessel the *Dash*, often referred to as the "Ghost Ship of Casco Bay," during the War of 1812 that sailed out of Porters' Landing in nearby Freeport. Both of them perished when the ship was lost in 1815.

In early October 1970, Leighton Tavern had its roof removed, its fireplaces disassembled and was sawed in half. Over a matter of days, the sections and pieces of the building were moved to its new home at Schooner Rocks on Cumberland Foreside. The tavern is now an elegant ocean-side private residence on Broad Cove.

Leighton Tavern, Cumberland. *Author photo.*

ALMOST EVERY TOWN IN the southern and coastal areas of the District of Maine had one or more taverns or inns. Many of these taverns served as local post offices. Taverns were located about eight to ten miles apart on the Old Post Road. The post riders had to exchange horses at these intervals, and they went inside the taverns to warm up and get something to eat and drink as they waited for the next post rider along the route to arrive and continue along the way.

It was Benjamin Franklin who established "post roads." These roads were improved to accommodate stagecoaches, and they developed rapidly to carry not only the mail and parcels but passengers as well, all of which provided more customers for the taverns. Many sections of the main road coming from Boston through Maine were labeled post roads. Once the roads were improved enough for stagecoaches, the post riders ceased operations, but the stagecoaches continued delivering packages, passengers and mail. Since these stagecoaches were pulled by horses, the teams of horses could travel only at the rate of four or five miles an hour with a change of horses

Concord Coach. *Collections of Scarborough Historical Society & Museum, MHS 29386.*

every eight to ten miles. Horses that pulled the stages one day could not pull another the very next day. They needed rest. So, other fresh horses that were in stables attached to the taverns or nearby had to be used. These stables most often had more than a dozen horses ready to do the job.

While there were several companies building stagecoaches, including companies in Albany and Troy, New York, the most common stagecoaches used in Maine were the Concord Coaches. Concord, New Hampshire, became the center for coach production in New England and down the East Coast. Concord Coach began when wheelwright Lewis Downing joined his skills with expert coachbuilder J. Stephens Abbot of Maine in 1926. Their partnership lasted over twenty years, turning into a thriving, world-renowned business. What separated Abbot and Downing from other coachbuilders of the day were the vehicles' handsome appearance, durability and overall quality. These masterpieces of construction had no equal. The Concord stagecoaches were the first to offer shock-absorbing through braces—an important feature not just for passengers but for the animals pulling them too. These braces allowed the coach to rock back and forth and swing sideways, providing forward momentum for the teams of horses. This feature allowed the coach to work up its own momentum when it was mired in a slough of bad road, of which Maine had plenty!

Concord Coaches came in three sizes built to hold six, nine or twelve passengers. They were usually drawn by teams of four horses, although the larger coaches required six. It is important to note that the coach itself was very small, and that is why most passengers did not sit inside but on top. It was only a bit over four feet in width, and its height inside was about four and a half feet. While the interior seats were upholstered in padded leather and damask cloth, the seats were reported to be harder than the wood beneath them.

The stagecoaches stopped at taverns and inns where the teams could be changed out and a meal could be gotten, then stagecoaches could travel along their way. Most stagecoach drivers stayed in the taverns and inns overnight and continued along their routes the next day. The ride was very bumpy, and the stagecoaches were not heated, so the passengers were eager for the opportunity to refresh themselves at the taverns along the way. It cost the equivalent of two days' pay to travel those eight to ten miles.

THE PRINCE TAVERN, CUMBERLAND (1820S–PRESENT)

The Prince Tavern is located at the intersection of what is now Tuttle Road and Main Street (Route 9) sitting diagonally across from the Congregational church.

James Prince bought the land the tavern sits on from Jeremiah Powell. It contained several lots, one of which was sold for use as a burial ground,

Prince Tavern, Cumberland. *Author photo.*

now the Congregational Cemetery. Ownership of one of the remaining lots where the tavern is located was transferred to James's son Joel, who became proprietor of the Prince Tavern. The main road at the time ran under the archway of the tavern/stables that you can see at the left of the photograph. Stagecoaches stopped and horses were changed from a stable of fifteen stalls, and overnight travelers stayed in the rooms upstairs over the tavern. Joel Prince sold the tavern to Nathaniel Blanchard in 1829, and in 1833, Nathaniel sold it to Captain Enos Blanchard. Enos's son George, who became the owner in 1874, ran the tavern until his son Arthur became owner upon George's death in 1935. In 1974, the tavern was sold to Dr. William Wyatt, who ran his practice there until it was converted to a coffee shop known locally as Doc's Place. The stable area of the tavern is now apartments. The former Prince Tavern is now the home of the Cumberland Food Company, a very successful coffee shop, café and market run by Bryan Dame and Kelsey Pettengill.

THE BUXTON TAVERN, NORTH YARMOUTH (1700S–PRESENT)

The Buxton Tavern, known as the Red House, was built in the late 1700s. The tavern catered to stagecoach passengers, drovers and peddlers. Horses were cared for in the tavern's stables.

After fourteen years, it was sold with "the buildings thereon" to twenty-seven-year-old Jeremiah Buxton in 1795. By that time, the county road from Yarmouth village to New Gloucester had been well established; six years later, it would intersect with the Hallowell Road directly in front of the Red House. Anyone traveling farther inland and along the stagecoach line that ran through the village was sure to pass by the Red House. The Buxtons also operated the post office for the Walnut Hill Village area of North Yarmouth.

Jeremiah Buxton married twenty-four-year-old Jane Drinkwater in 1796, and by 1797, they had established a tavern and inn at the North Yarmouth location. They also farmed the property and raised cattle. Their eldest son, William, took after his industrious parents. At age seventeen, he joined the family business and eventually held railroad stocks with Jeremiah, along with shares in Union Wharf in Yarmouth, where cargo from ships was unloaded to be carried by horse-driven wagons northwest to Auburn and points beyond. He also owned shares in a stagecoach line carrying passengers that

Buxton Tavern, North Yarmouth. *Author photo.*

ran through Walnut Hill Village. Jeremiah Jr., son of Jeremiah, ran the Red House tavern for many years after it was passed along to him by his parents.

The Buxton family businesses catered to the traveler. At this busy intersection, the family offered a store, blacksmith shop and cooperage, which son Edward operated. People on their way through Walnut Hill traveling north and west were following the road to Hallowell (Route 9) or were on their way to Gray and farther to New Gloucester, a courthouse site. Going south and east, they were making their way to Yarmouth or Portland with goods to sell. One or two stagecoach routes also passed through here. Stagecoach passengers stayed in the Red House. The cattle drovers and peddlers did not stay at the tavern but stayed nearby. After passing down through the family for many years, the tavern, along with thirty acres, was eventually sold to neighbor Samuel H. Sweetser. The house is now a private residence.

It was customary for the stage to arrive at an inn at the hour of noon, when the heartiest meal of the day was served. When it came to overnight stay in the earliest days at these taverns and inns, there was no such thing as a private room or indoor bathroom. All beds were large enough to accommodate at least two people, and frequently there were as many as three beds in a room. The tavern keeper did not consider his house filled until every bed was yielding at least double income. If a guest wanted a bath or fire in the fireplace or stove in the room, there was an extra charge of about a half day's pay at the time. The fire was kindled to order, and the bath was taken in their room in a wooden tub, which a porter filled with hot water carried up from the kitchen.

The stagecoach succumbed to the competition of the railroads by the 1820s. The first railroad cars resembled the stagecoaches in many ways. The earliest passenger cars on the railroads were nothing more than stagecoaches reassembled to travel on tracks pulled by steam engines to replace the pulling power of horses. This is why you see so many of the taverns and inns in Maine located near railroad lines.

TAVERN LIFE IN EARLY MAINE

The Jameson Tavern, Freeport (1779–Present)

The Jameson Tavern at 115 Main Street in Freeport was built in 1779 by Dr. John Anglier Hyde and was sold to Captain Samuel Jameson almost immediately. There are no records indicating Dr. Hyde ever lived in the house. Captain Jameson and his wife ran it as Jameson's Tavern from 1801 until the widow Jameson sold it in 1828. During this period, Freeport was a key stagecoach town located between Portland and the towns and cities farther up the Maine coast. Henry Wadsworth Longfellow and John Greenleaf Whittier stayed at Jameson's Tavern, as did President Franklin Pierce. The inn was a popular meeting place for all the prominent businessmen in the area, and the taproom was known for its "fine spirits and jovial atmosphere."

The newspapers of that time indicate it was a favorite meeting place for many years during the time the District of Maine was pursuing independence from Massachusetts. Freeport was a shipping port, and the goods that were on these ships were heavily taxed by Massachusetts, so one of the goals of those seeking independence was to alleviate the tax burden. The idea of separation was an extremely controversial issue within the District of Maine at that time. A good percentage of the population felt the connection to Boston was essential for future business.

Allegedly, the commissioners met on the northeast corner of the second floor of Jameson's Tavern to sign the final papers giving Maine its

Jameson Tavern, Freeport. *Author photo.*

independence from Massachusetts, thus giving the town of Freeport and Jameson's Tavern their right to claim as the "Birthplace of Maine." A plaque was placed on the property of Jameson's Tavern in 1914 by the Daughters of the American Revolution commemorating this historic event. Maine entered the Union through the Missouri Compromise, which admitted Maine as a free state and Missouri as a slave state.

In 1828, the widow Jameson sold the inn to Richard Codman, and it became known as Codman's Tavern. Codman continued to run it as an inn and tavern until 1856.

In 1856, the property was purchased by John Cushing, a local shipbuilder from Porters Landing in Freeport. Cushing redecorated the house into the Victorian style of the times, with the exception of the one room where the commissioners had met thirty-six years earlier. The original state of the tavern is borne out by both the window seats and molding in one of the rooms, as well as the name "J.C. Cushing" scratched into one of the old panes of glass.

After Cushing's ownership, the house fell into some disrepair due to neglect, passing from family to family until the current owners purchased it in 1981. An attempt was made to restore the house to what it would most likely have looked like in 1779, without the advantage of original records. The old panes of glass can still be seen in many of the original windows. You can still see framed rubbings from the tombstones of Dr. Hyde and Captain Jameson in the front halls of the tavern.

The following is an excerpt of an interesting paper written and read by Mrs. Edwin A. Richardson, past regent of Elizabeth Wadsworth Chapter DAR, at the unveiling of the plaque placed on the Old Jameson Tavern on September 1, 1915, by the Daughters of the American Revolution of Maine.

Maine's Independence

Among all the interesting old houses in Maine there is none of more importance, from an historical standpoint than the old tavern at Freeport in which were signed the final papers separating Maine from Massachusetts. Built a century and a quarter ago, for Dr. John Hyde of Freeport, it was his home for many years. Later it passed out of the possession of the worthy doctor's descendants, and for a long period of time was used as a public house. At the time of the Commissioners' meeting in Freeport it was known as the Jameson Tavern, later it became the Codman Tavern, and still later it was called the Elm House.

Following this, the old house returned to its original standing, and became once more a private dwelling house, the home of Charles Cushing, a prominent ship builder of the town. It next passed into the possession of the present owner, Mrs. Frank R. Kennedy of Portland, Me.

The act of separation, which was finally consummated in this old tavern, took place on the 15th day of March 1820, and on that date, Maine became a State and took the honored place that was rightfully hers in the Union. The movement for the separation of Maine from Massachusetts began soon after the Revolutionary period, and the matter was largely agitated by the most patriotic men of the district at intervals for a period of over thirty years. Eminent statesmen devoted much time and energy to this end, and when it was announced that the papers were actually signed which constituted Maine a free and independent State, great enthusiasm was manifested by those who advocated the movement.

This old tavern was one of the favorite stopping places for the big stages that journeyed between the eastern part of the province of Maine and Massachusetts. It was chosen by the commissioners for their meeting because it was a convenient location, while its reputation of serving the best food and the best New England rum of any tavern on the old Boston and Maine highway, may not have been overlooked by the commissioners when they ratified the act of separation.

In subsequent years, several reputable historians, including historians at the Freeport Historical Society, have disputed the town's claim as the Birthplace of Maine. The legend survives, however, that a meeting did, indeed, take place at the tavern in 1820 when separation papers were signed to establish a separate state of Maine.

THE KING TAVERN, BATH (1910–1926)

The King Tavern was originally the residence of William King, Maine's first governor. After King's death in 1852, the building was moved to its Vine Street location to make room for the Federal Building, which was completed in 1858. King's former residence served as a tavern and hotel under a variety of names until destroyed in 1926. It was known as the King Tavern from 1910 to 1926. In 1926, the building was torn down to provide space for the Vine Street approach to the Carlton Bridge.

Governor King was significant in not only Bath's history but Maine's history, as well. William King was born to Richard King, a merchant and shipowner, and Mary Black on February 9, 1768, at Scarborough, then in the Province of Massachusetts Bay. William King was employed in a variety of businesses, including as a shipbuilder and then as a ship owner. He became the largest merchant shipping owner in Maine. He was a successful merchant and a significant real estate investor. He opened the first cotton mill in Maine in nearby Brunswick and also founded and was the president of the first bank of Bath. But it was his political career that is most significant. In 1705, he became a member of the Democratic-Republican Party, representing nearby Topsham in the Massachusetts House of Representatives in 1795 and 1799. The Democratic-Republican Party, originally the Republican Party (1792–98), was the first opposition political party in the United States. It was organized in 1792 as the Republican Party and was the direct antecedent of the present Democratic Party. Upon moving to Bath in 1804, King represented that town as well and later was elected to serve in the Massachusetts Senate from 1807 to 1811.

King Tavern. *Collections of Patten Free Library, MHS 10527.*

When the War of 1812 broke out, Massachusetts made him a major general of the militia in charge of the Maine District, where he used his shipbuilding knowledge to attend to coastal shipping and defenses. King also led recruiting efforts for the regular army, for which he was made a colonel. In 1813, King began a seven-year effort that started with his petition to Massachusetts for the separation of the District of Maine. In 1816, he was reelected to the Massachusetts Senate and was the most significant citizen of the District of Maine in securing approval for Maine to become a separate state, which was granted as part of the Missouri Compromise on March 15, 1820. He was shortly elected as Maine's first governor. Just one year later, President James Monroe named him one of the three commissioners to settle land claims from the 1819 Adams-Onis Treaty. This treaty was the agreement between the United States and Spain that established the southern border of the Louisiana Territory. As part of the agreement, the United States obtained the territory of present-day Florida.

King resigned as governor in 1821 to take the position of U.S. commissioner, serving until 1824. In 1828, he was appointed by President Andrew Jackson to serve as customs collector of Bath. He was the signatory on the petition to have Maine become a separate state while he was living in what became later known as the King Tavern, and a statue of King is now on prominent display in the Statutory Hall in Washington, D.C. The statue was accepted in the collection by Senator Hannibal Hamlin, who himself became the subject of Maine's second entry to the collection, and Senator James G. Blaine on January 22, 1878. Blaine rhapsodized about King on the occasion: "He restrained the wrath of the impudent, quickened the zeal of the laggard, dissipated the fears of the doubting and molded his adherents and followers into a compact, cooperative, effective force....He, more than any other man created the State of Maine."

AS STATED IN THE introduction, Maine was part of Massachusetts until statehood was granted in 1820. Up until that time, life was hard. The taverns and houses built were simple, with timber frames covered in clapboard and thatched or rough sawn shingle roofs. Most could not afford to have glass imported from England, so they used sheets of paper or canvas soaked in oil to cover their windows. The chimneys were of logs covered in plaster and often caused fires that consumed most or all of the structures. The houses were dark and very drafty, as well. About the mid- to late 1700s, more substantial structures were being built as the citizens became more prosperous. They added more rooms to their taverns and houses and replaced the oil paper or canvas with glass in their windows and the dirt floors with those made of wood.

Inns, at that time, provided a place to stay as well as eat and drink, though typically accommodations were concerned with quantity and not quality. Only the very rich could afford a private room, if one were even available. A meal often cost more than the lodging for those sharing a bed with a stranger or companion, which was a common practice in early taverns. You could also expect to pay more for clean linens. In the more remote areas of the District of Maine, you might very well find yourself sleeping on the floor, accompanied by rats, mice and fleas.

ROBERT ROSE TAVERN, YORK (1750S–PRESENT)

The Robert Rose Tavern is a historic house and former tavern at 298 Long Sands. Built in the 1750s using elements of a house built in 1680, it is one of the oldest surviving public hostelries (lodgings) in the state. The original house was built by John Banks, one of York's early settlers.

Robert Rose Tavern, York. *Author photo.*

The property on which the tavern stands was granted to John Banks, the son of Richard Banks, who settled in York in 1642. John Banks, born in York in 1657, built his house in 1680. Banks and his house survived the 1692 Candlemas Massacre in which his father and two brothers perished, probably because it was set well back from the beach. The raid took place on January 24, 1692, during King William's War when Chief Madockawando and Father Louis-Pierre Thury led two to three hundred Natives into the town of York in the District of Maine, part of the Province of Massachusetts Bay, killing about one hundred of the English settlers and burning down buildings, taking another estimated eighty villagers hostage.

In 1756, Robert Rose purchased the Banks property and built the present house as a major expansion of Banks's 1680 house, leaving little more than parts of the frame and foundation as recognizably seventeenth century in origin. Rose operated the tavern until 1782 and was active in local civic affairs, hosting meetings of the town selectmen. He supplemented his income by working as the keeper of the local jail. Now a private residence, the house was listed in the National Register of Historic Places in 1979.

In the days before an understanding of bacteria and purification, colonists believed water unhealthy since it often made them sick. Alcoholic drinks were served at meals not only to adults but to children as well. Children were often served cider with their meals. The wealthier imported wine and brandy. The types of drinks found in taverns varied anywhere from beers and ciders to teas, wines and mixed concoctions. Hard liquor was common for those of British descent, although German inhabitants preferred beer. Rum was cheap and became the favorite drink served in taverns. The typical colonist in the late seventeenth century drank almost four gallons of hard liquor each year. Water was foul, infected and generally suspect, so the tavern-goers chased all the hard liquor with gallons of beer, rum, cider and wine.

The most universal staple in all colonial taverns was rum. A liquor unique to the colonies, rum originated from the gypsy word for "powerful," and the effects of it corroborated. Rum was such an important part of the average diet that even supplying it to the poor was an acceptable practice. The more well-to-do stocked it in their homes along with their flour and molasses. Tavern owners sold it by the glass and kept a "grog score" in their ledgers for frequent customers. Workmen of the day often would accept rum as part of payment for their services, and it was common to see rum expensed on itemized bills for tradesmen. Drinking rum was a way of life during the colonial days. Rum became such a popular drink before the American Revolutionary War that it is estimated that every man, woman or child was drinking an average of 3.6 gallons of rum each year. Two of the most popular drinks in colonial taverns were flip and punch. Flip, a distinctly American beverage, was made in pitchers and consisted of two-thirds strong beer sweetened with sugar, molasses or dried pumpkin and rum. Into this mixture was dropped a red-hot iron loggerhead that made it foam and gave the drink its unique burnt, bitter taste. Punch was another popular drink in colonial America that had its origins in India. The basic recipe for the drink was the combination of tea, rum, arrack (fermented coconut sugar), sugar, lemons and water in a large bowl. Taverns often had several of their own distinct versions of punch that were classified by various other fruit juices, liquors and spices as well as the quantities of each used.

Many of the early settlers turned their barley fields into apple orchards, growing a variety of apples to press into cider to sell to local markets and taverns. The climate in the District of Maine was ideal for growing apples because of the cold, crisp weather. Many orchard owners began the production of hard cider as the orchards matured. By the early eighteenth century, production had become so successful that even small villages of fifty families or fewer could press and ferment more than three thousand barrels of hard cider each growing season. Cider was the choice of many for breakfast, lunch and dinner. They not only served hard cider to drink, but they also used it in cooking baked ham and sometimes even chicken. If the tavern owner was not brewing his own beer or hard cider, he bought it from a local brewer, and very often, the tavern owner would press this cider and ferment it into apple brandy.

Here is the recipe for one tavern owner's punch:

> *"Fish House Punch."*
> *Dissolve ¾ pounds of sugar into a punch bowl filled with a bottle of lemon juice adding two bottles of rum, one bottle of cognac, two bottles of water, one wine glass of peach cordial, and a large block of ice and let this concoction stand about two hours before serving.*

Tavern-goers very often found themselves enjoying hasty pudding, and in the fall months, they often were served red flannel hash, which consisted of available meats stewed with potatoes, beets, cabbage, turnip, carrots and garlic vinegar. Some of the recipes used most likely came from *Hannah Glasse's Art of Cookery Made Plain & Simple*, a popular cookbook published in 1747.

Most of you have heard of hasty pudding. It was very popular and originated in England and was often served through the day in the taverns in the colonies. The original recipe for hasty pudding is as follows:

> *Put two quarts of water into a clean dinner pot or saucepan, cover it and let it become boiling hot over the fire; then add a teaspoon of salt, take off the light scum from the top, have secured to use some sweet fresh yellow or white corn meal. Take a handful of the meal with the left hand, and by degrees, let fall into the meal; when one handful is exhausted, refill it; continue to stir and add meal until it is as thick as you can stir easily, or until the stick will stand in it; stir it a little while longer; let the fire be gentle; when it is sufficiently cooked, which will be in a half an hour, it will bubble or puff; turn it into a deep basin. This is good eaten cold or hot, with milk or with butter and syrup or sugar, or with meat gravy, the same as potatoes or rice.*

Few people used forks in the early taverns, and it was common for two or more to share a wooden plate called a trencher. A trencher was generally oblong or square, and people ate directly from it, passing this rudimentary plate from person to person. Forks were seldom used, although many people had a couple of silver or pewter spoons, but wooden spoons were the most common. As mentioned previously, glass was a rare commodity. A bottle would be considered valuable, and you often see glass bottles mentioned in someone's will. Many of the wealthier colonists owned silver or pewter cups. Most of the common people drank from wooden goblet-type tankards constructed like small barrels or even tankards made from leather. Many homes had small bowls to hold soups and stews. Again, since tableware was scarce, many of these bowls had handles and had multiple uses. It was common for those sitting at the table to pass the tankards they used to drink from to others sharing the meal unless they brought their own drinking vessel. The bowls were for your own use, however, and not shared.

Hallowell House, Hallowell (1832–1959)

The town of Hallowell began construction of the Hallowell House in 1832 to try to keep up its competition with Augusta, which was chosen as the capital in 1830. This Federal period five-story building spanned eighty-four feet on Second Street in Hallowell and had seventy rooms, each with its own fireplace. The Hallowell House hosted highly esteemed visitors such as President Theodore Roosevelt and writers like Nathaniel Hawthorne and

Hallowell House, Hallowell. *Author collection.*

Henry Wadsworth Longfellow. The Hallowell House Hotel, Restaurant and Tavern continued to function throughout the years, accommodating famous visitors such as Margaret Chase Smith, a Maine native who was active in the U.S. House of Representatives and U.S. Senate. The Hallowell House closed in 1959 and was renovated into an apartment building.

THE BLACKHAWK PUTNAM TAVERN, HOULTON (1813–PRESENT)

The Blackhawk Putnam Tavern is a historic house at 22 North Street (U.S. Route 1) in Houlton. Built in 1813, it is Aroostook County's oldest standing building. In the mid-nineteenth century, it served as a tavern on the military road, and one of its owners was Blackhawk Putnam, a veteran of the American Civil War.

The tavern was built in 1813 by Samuel Wormwood, a master carpenter originally from Alfred, Maine, for Aaron Putnam, who had settled in the Houlton area in 1805. It was not the first house built in Houlton by Wormwood; a house built by him for the local doctor in 1812 burned down in 1879. Houlton was connected to the rest of Maine by a military road built in 1828, and it is probable that the house began to serve as a tavern around then, as it was likely the largest house in the small community. The house was the scene of several sessions of the Washington County District Court before the area was set off as Aroostook County in 1839. It then held sessions of the Washington County District Court for a number of

Blackhawk Tavern. Built in 1813, it is Aroostook County's oldest standing building. *Collections of Aroostook County Historical Society and Museum, MHS 16304.*

years and was owned by John Varnum Putnam, the county sheriff, for many years. Aaron Putnam's son Blackhawk commanded a company of Maine volunteer infantry in the American Civil War. The property was used as a restaurant for a time after Blackhawk's death; it is now a private residence. It was listed in the National Register of Historic Places on January 30, 1976.

TAVERNS HAVE ALWAYS PLAYED a crucial role in the community. These taverns served as gathering places for those in a community and as a respite for travelers, offering food and overnight lodging. The tavern owner typically lived on the premises in an area separated from the guests. Visitors staying overnight brought news and information from throughout the colonies. It was an effective means of communication, as it helped the settlers maintain contact with the countries and towns they migrated from. Taverns also served as the focus for an entire region, not just for the towns where they were located. Government buildings were virtually nonexistent, yet it was essential for officials to conduct business and maintain laws. The practical solution was to bring government to outlying areas by a system known as "riding the circuit." By using a tavern room, they were able to hold court without encumbering great expense. It was so successful that they soon assigned the tavern yet another duty, which was as a meeting place for the local militia.

RICHARD FITCH'S TAVERN, WEST BALDWIN (1785)

Richard Fitch's Tavern was built about 1785 in West Baldwin, where the first town meeting was held on August 30, 1802. The tavern immediately became a center for all gatherings. The militia in everyday homespun and their officers in uniform assembled to train or to start on their night march under Captain Edward Small for general muster in Raymond. The first post office was established at the tavern with Richard Fitch as postmaster.

The selectmen from the town of Baldwin, Josiah Pierce, William Fitch and Nathan Sawyer, were in session at Richard Fitch's Tavern on February 15, 1819. The selectmen were assembled to qualify additional inhabitants of the town to be included on the current list of voters for town officers.

The selectmen, including Pierce, Fitch and Lot Davis, requested constable John Burnell to notify the qualified Baldwin voters to meet at Richard Fitch's Tavern on July 26, 1819, to decide who would represent Baldwin at the Maine Constitutional Convention in Portland on October 14, 1819, and to decide the question of whether the District of Maine should separate from Massachusetts and become an independent state. Seventy-nine votes were cast; fifty-three voted in favor of separation, and twenty-six voted against separation.

Threats to a town came from a variety of places, and protection was needed for survival. It was up to the colonists to provide their own defense by having a volunteer militia. Thrifty governors, knowing it was difficult for colonists to attend the mandatory militia training, found a simple solution by designating a tavern as the meeting place and providing a free keg of beer.

The Spear Tavern (Early 1700s)

The Spear Tavern in Brunswick was built in the early 1700s and was operated by Robert Spear between 1744 and 1760. The inn was also a garrison house protected by timber fortification, and soldiers were kept there by the government for the safety of travelers and for the protection of the citizens. It was used as a public house after the Fifth Indian War, which was the culmination of a continuing dispute between England and France. The period was marked by a series of Indian raids on white settlements who had the active support of the French interested in seeing the English settlers driven from the land. One of the significant military developments of the French and Indian Wars was the capture of the French fort at Louisburg, Nova Scotia, in 1745 by a contingent of forces led by William Pepperell of Kittery. Town meetings were frequently held in this tavern, and in cold weather, the tavern was a popular stop for people who wanted a warm place to meet for lunch and grog after Sunday church services.

The Thompson Tavern, Brunswick/Topsham (About 1750)

The Thompson Tavern was built in about 1750. James Thompson opened a tavern on a farm located in the New Meadows area. The tavern was kept by Thompson's son Brigadier Samuel Thompson, who ran it until 1784. Samuel Thompson led the early American Revolutionary War confrontation between Samuel Thompson's Patriot militia, who met and trained at the tavern, and Loyalists supported by the British warship the HMS *Canceaux*. The confrontation ended without fatalities but provoked the burning of Falmouth, later renamed Portland, five months later. Samuel Thompson was elected commander of the Brunswick militia in 1774 and headed the local enforcement committee for the Continental Association created by the First Continental Congress to boycott all goods from Great Britain. The Continental Association was formed to enforce the boycott on March 2, 1775, against a shipload of sail, rope and rigging for Loyalist Captain Samuel Coulson of Falmouth (now Portland) by demanding the delivery ship leave port. The HMS *Canceaux* was dispatched from Boston, and following its arrival on March 29, Coulson proceeded to offload his British goods under the protection of the British warship. The Battles of Lexington and Concord took place ninety miles to the south while the *Canceaux* lay at anchor in Casco Bay. When news of the battle reached Brunswick on April 21, the Brunswick Militia, led by Thompson, laid plans to capture the HMS *Canceaux*. Fifty Brunswick militiamen wearing sprigs of spruce in their hats as a uniform arrived in Portland secretly on small boats carrying a spruce tree with the lower branches cleared away as a battle ensign. The HMS *Canceaux* was prepared to prevent those in small boats from boarding, but Thompson's militia captured the warship's captain, Lieutenant Henry Mowat, on May 9, 1775, while he was ashore arranging for church services for his crew. The first lieutenant aboard the HMS *Canceaux* discharged two cannon salutes, which are gunpowder charges without shot, toward Portland and threatened to shell Portland unless the captain was released. Six hundred militiamen from surrounding communities gathered as Portland residents negotiated to prevent their community from becoming a battleground. Mowat was allowed to return to his ship, but his demand to arrest Thompson was refused, and the assembled militia forced the HMS *Canceaux* to leave port on May 15. Disappointed militiamen vented their frustration by looting the homes of Coulson and Loyalist Sheriff Tyng before returning to their inland communities. News of Thompson's attempt encouraged Machias

Thompson Tavern, Brunswick/Topsham. *Author photo.*

militiamen to capture the British armed schooner *Margaretta* a month later in the Battle of Machias. Mowat brought the HMS *Canceaux* back to Portland in October to set fire to the city, which left Portland's population homeless as winter approached. The Massachusetts House of Representatives promoted Samuel Thompson to brigadier of the Cumberland County Militia on February 8, 1776, in recognition of his initiative following the Battles of Lexington and Concord, and the spruce trees his men carried provided inspiration for adoption of the Pine Tree Flag as the Massachusetts naval ensign in April 1776.

You often hear the words *tavern*, *inn* and *ordinary*. The difference between a colonial-era tavern and an inn is that the inn offered accommodation, while the tavern only food and drink. The word *ordinary* was used in the 1600s and 1700s to mean the same as tavern. By the mid-eighteenth century, the word *tavern* had become the common name, and you rarely heard them referred to as ordinaries from that point on.

MILLIKEN'S TAVERN, SCARBOROUGH (LATE 1700S–PRESENT)

Milliken's Tavern was a popular tavern, inn and stable used by those traveling by stagecoach and was built in the late 1700s. It is located on Route 1 in Scarborough just north of the Saco town line, which was then referred to as the King's Highway and later the Post Road. The tavern was one of several structures on a large farm. There were also mills on the property. Water for travelers and horses was pumped from Stuart's Brook, a tributary of the Scarborough River that runs through the property. The brick building shown in this photo replaced the original structure in 1815.

The tavern was originally owned by Captain Mulberry Milliken, who was in the shipping business with Richard King. Captain Benjamin Milliken, Mulberry's son, ran the inn for his father. The tavern business began to decline when the railroad between Boston and Portland began in 1840. The building that housed the tavern was purchased by Silas Lary in 1875 and was used as a private residence from that point on.

BEAL'S TAVERN, NORWAY (1871–1960S)

Beal's Tavern began as Beal's Hotel in 1871 when Ezra Beal purchased a residence a few years earlier. He added two stories to the residence and opened a thirty-room tavern/inn that was run by his son George Lafayette Beal. George Lafayette Beal is one of Norway's most famous residents, having distinguished himself during the Civil War when he rose to the rank of brevet general. He only managed the tavern/inn for a short while, however, relinquishing running the tavern when he was appointed U.S. pension agent and later the treasurer of the state.

The tavern/inn had a tough run and was barely profitable over the years. The tavern was leased several times in the years subsequent to George L. Beal's management. In 1888, the Beal's Hotel Corp. was formed, made up of local citizens who saw the need for a public house. Several prominent men were shareholders, including George L. Beal, who held the majority of shares. The corporation repaired the building and refurnished it. In 1893, William K. Bickford of Thomaston leased/managed the tavern/inn. In 1897, the corporation sold the tavern/inn to John Woodman, who ran it for thirteen years. In 1910, it was sold to Simeon Conrad. It was then sold in

Milliken's Tavern, Scarborough. *Author photo.*

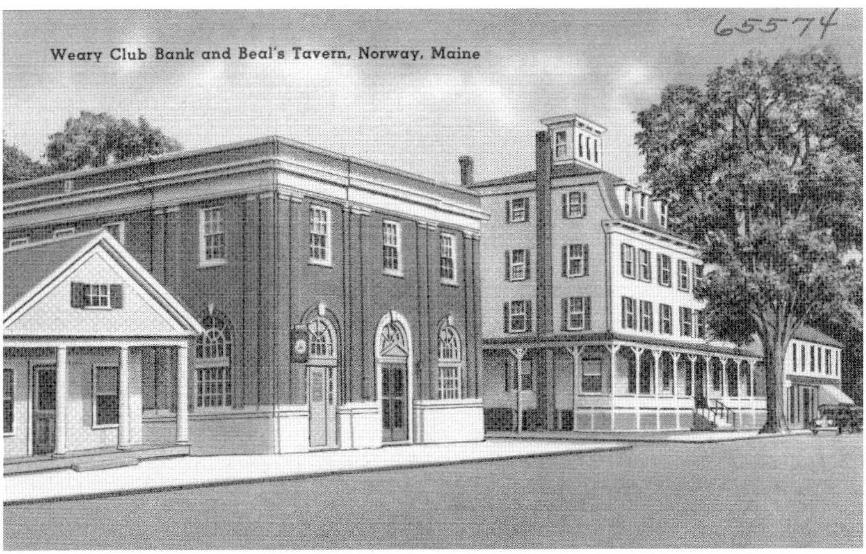

Beal's Tavern. *Collections of Boston Public Library, MHS 68663.*

1913 to Robert Seavey, who renamed it Beal's Inn and then Beal's Tavern. In 1943, Seavey sold to William Davis of Portland. During the time Seavey owned it, he closed the dining room, but the guest rooms remained open. When William Davis became the owner, he reopened the dining room and redecorated it. Dining room capacity was about seventy-five diners.

Davis owned it until 1949, when it was sold to Josephine and Ralph Stone of Norway, who ran it as the Hotel Stone until 1961. Josephine Stone was a locally famous and much-honored restaurateur who ran a restaurant farther up Main Street for more than fifty years, circa 1930s to circa 1990s. She was a generous philanthropist who preferred to remain anonymous.

During its existence, the hotel catered to traveling salesmen and summer visitors. After the Stones bought it in 1949, they also provided some of the rooms to elderly people for a very low rate, which included meals. When the Stones decided to close in 1961, they found new accommodations for the elderly residents. Josephine Stone is quoted as noting that as time went on, traveling salesmen were given company cars so they would return home each night rather than stay in a hotel. That, and more modern motels being built around Norway, led to the decision to close the hotel. The tavern/inn was torn down, and only a parking lot remains where it once stood.

Maine communities and taverns were established early in Maine's history. York, Saco and Cape Porpoise were established in 1630; Kittery and Scarborough in 1631; Falmouth in 1633; North Yarmouth in 1636; and Wells in 1642, and by the late 1700s, they started establishing taverns in those towns. The settlers took advantage of coastal salt marshes to expand their herds of cattle and sheep, and they worked in seasonal trades like fishing, lumbering, milling, seafaring and trapping. The vast salt marshes were covered in summer with grass and were a great feed source for cattle and sheep. Women settlers in the early seventeenth century stayed closer to home in their kitchens, barnyard, orchards and milk-houses. Milk-houses are buildings used for the cooling, handling and bottling of milk. Some women specialized in producing yarn, fabric, dairy products or crafts that they traded with or sold to neighbors to supplement their incomes.

ALICE GREELE'S TAVERN, PORTLAND (EARLY 1700S TO 1846)

Alice Greele's Tavern was built in the early 1700s. This tavern was located on the corner of what is now Congress and Hampshire Streets in Portland. Greele's Tavern was significant in the history of Maine during the American Revolution. The building was small for a tavern, one story and long. Because the tavern was one of the few buildings downtown that survived the bombing by the British, it became a sort of headquarters for Falmouth (now Portland) during the Revolutionary War.

Here is a quote from *Historic Towns of New England:*

> *The fashionable tavern of the town was kept by Dame Alice Greele, and here, during the whole Revolutionary period, the committee of public safety met, the judges held their courts, and political conventions had their sessions. It was here that the citizens in town meeting heroically voted to stand the bombardment rather than give up the guns demanded by Mowatt. But after making this brave decision they hastily packed up all their portable possessions and removed their families to places for safety, some traveling as far as to islands in Casco Bay, and others finding shelter under the lee*

Alice Greele's Tavern. *Collections of Maine Historical Society, MHS 22428.*

of a high cliff that used to be at the corner of Casco and Cumberland Streets, at no great distance from their homes. Braver than the bravest men of Falmouth, Dame Alice would not desert her tavern, although its position was so dangerously exposed that every house in its vicinity was destroyed by bursting bombs and heated cannon-balls. Throughout that terrible day she stood at her post, and with buckets of water extinguished the fires on her premises as fast as they were kindled. When Mowatt's ships began to throw red-hot cannon-balls, one of them fell into the dame's back yard among some chips, which were set on fire. She picked up the ball in a pan, and as she tossed it into the street, she said to a neighbor who was passing: "They will have to stop firing soon, for they have got out of bombs and are making new balls and can't wait for them to cool!" Over the years, Portland's leaders have talked about placing a bronze tablet at the site of Alice Greele's tavern, but it has not happened yet. The building stood until 1846 at the corner of Congress and Hampshire Streets. It was then removed to Washington Street.

On October 18, 1775, the community was destroyed yet again, bombarded for nine hours by the British navy's HMS *Canceaux* under the command of Lieutenant Henry Mowatt. The burning of Falmouth left three-quarters of the town in ashes and its citizens committed to independence. When rebuilt, the community's center shifted from India Street to where the Old Port district is today.

AS MENTIONED PREVIOUSLY, ONE of the main reasons for taverns during the early years was as a social/government hub. Issues of the day were discussed and hammered out there often in official settings. The City Tavern in Philadelphia, for example, was the site of the first Continental Congress, and the Virginia legislature met in the taverns of Williamsburg. The Salem witch trials were supposed to be held at Ingersoll's Ordinary, though in the end it was too small for the crowds. Taverns in the District of Maine served similar purposes. It was in Maine taverns that the locals learned what the current prices were for their cash crops and products, and it was where they could find a newspaper that was often read aloud since more than half of the citizens could not read at that time. But it was also a place where neighbors met to simply talk and play games. Some of the games played in taverns during this period were chess and checkers. Checkers was known as *check* during that time in our history. The earliest colonists used kernels of corn when playing checkers. Backgammon was considered a game for the elite.

Gaming occurred often in taverns, and it was a controversial issue, not because of the games themselves but rather for the gambling that surrounded them. Card games and darts were very popular in taverns. But outside games were also played. Cricket, sometimes referred to as quoits, was played, as was the game of ninepins, an early form of bowling, often occurring in side alleys. Cockfighting was also popular, but just like the card games, the gambling surrounding cockfighting was frowned upon, and many communities tried to control this, without much success. Those participating and the tavern owners faced the possibility of fines and imprisonment.

The Broad Tavern, Stroudwater (1780s–1922)

Thaddeus Broad (1744–1824), of Natick, Massachusetts, came to Cape Elizabeth in 1771 and worked at Samuel Skillings's saw- and gristmill at Long Creek. He married Samuel's daughter Lucy (1753–1837) that same year, and they had at least eleven children who made it into adulthood.

In the early 1770s, Thaddeus was renting land from Isaac Winslow on the Boston Road in Stroudwater, now Westbrook Street, and built a small home. As early as 1780, he is listed as an innkeeper. In 1782, he bought the land from Winslow and built the Broad Tavern. It appears the saltbox feature was added later, with a hall, dining room and bowling alley. A couple of sources give the building date of the tavern as 1786; that may be when the saltbox was added. Until the bridges to Cape Elizabeth were built, all land travel between Portland and Boston passed this way. Broad stimulated trade by erecting a platform with a railing in a large elm that stood in front of the tavern. A stairway was built to this nest where liquor was served to customers, and soon the elm came to be known as the Bar Room Tree. When General Lafayette stopped at Broad's for liquid refreshment on his way from Portland in 1825, he was served at this aerial bar. From that time, the tree was called the Lafayette Elm. Customers at the tavern were allowed many privileges besides that of eating and drinking, and men with a flair for gambling often played cards until the early hours of the morning.

Broad Tavern. *Collections of Maine Historical Society, MHS 40332.*

One Saturday evening, such a game was in progress, but at midnight, one of the players, more impish than righteous, suggested that they set aside the winnings accumulated during the hours of the Sabbath and present the "tainted money" to Parson Caleb Bradley; they thought this would be a great joke on the parson. Unwilling to wait until daylight to gloat over the parson's dilemma, they went to his house at about four o'clock in the morning and thumped loudly on his door to wake him. Startled out of his warm bed at such an ungodly hour, he stumbled to the door. The young men gave him the money, explaining in detail that, inasmuch as they had won it by gambling, they did not think it proper to keep it. They asked him if he would please accept it and then rushed away rather than face the good man's wrath. To their utter amazement, the parson shouted after them, "That's right, boys! That is right! The devil's money will buy just as many Bibles as God's money. Why didn't you play longer?"

Thaddeus Broad's son Silas (1795–1873) was host at the tavern until dwindling returns forced him out of business in about 1840. The house and 120-acre farm were sold in 1875 to Mary Jones, who was apparently related in some way. Thaddeus's oldest daughter Margaret married Captain John

Jones. Thaddeus's granddaughter Almira Ann Broad (1820–1903) was the grantee of the property and may have lived there later and even reopened the tavern in 1880 for a couple years. The Lafayette Elm was blown down in a storm in 1882. Retired Portland fire chief Nahum Littlefield took a big section of it back to his shop and carved an intricate chair that is on display at the Portland Fire Museum on Spring Street.

In 1892, Mary Jones, living in Philadelphia, sold the tavern and farm to brothers Frank P. and Elmer E. Cummings, who owned Cummings Bros. wholesale grocers in Portland. Sometime between 1898 and 1924, it lost its saltbox addition, which it appears was not original to the 1782 house. In 1922, Elmer Cummings retired and moved to Brooksville. At that time, he sold the tavern to Central Maine Development Company, which planned to develop it into over two hundred house lots called Bay Shore. A portion of this land was used to develop what is now the Portland International Jetport. A handful of those lots, which included the old tavern and barn, were sold that year to George W. Mills, who later bought a few more. A few other lots sold, mostly down on the Fore River, and a road named Broadway was built down to the river, just north of the old tavern.

AUNT PEPPERMINT'S TAVERN, NORTH HAVEN (MID-1800S)

Aunt Peppermint's Tavern, also referred to as the Banks House or Bush Tavern, was an interesting place in operation on a small island in Penobscot Bay just off Rockland in the mid-1800s. Today, the island has fewer than 355 year-round residents and is accessed by either a ferry from Rockland or air taxi from Knox County Regional Airport. What makes this tavern interesting is that it was most likely a house of prostitution as well, according to research done by Barbara (Beverage) Reeves, a descendant, and published in 2005 in a booklet titled *The Saga of the Banks's House or Bush Tavern*. The North Haven Historical Society has a copy of this booklet. "Tales of Aunt Peppermint" (named after peppermint extract, which was more than 90 percent alcohol) said that the person she most favored was likely one of Billy Banks's daughters, who reportedly ran the tavern with her sisters. Others report the tavern was run by Billy himself and provided "sisters" for warmth and companionship. The tavern was only in operation for a few years, but there must have been plenty of stories to tell.

Dancing was discouraged in early New England, including Maine, because of religious beliefs. By the 1800s, however, dancing had become acceptable and was very popular in taverns and inns. Formal activities were also held in taverns. Concerts, dinners, receptions and even balls were held in taverns. Taverns also booked traveling freak shows, like you see at modern-day fairs and carnivals, and those promoting new inventions set up in taverns, as well. The first lottery games in America were found in taverns, but they were strictly regulated by town leaders. And, of course, taverns were favorite spots for those running for office to campaign. Since there were few town halls, many of the first elections in America took place in taverns.

Captain Seth Spring Tavern, Biddeford (1798–Present)

A regular stopping point for travelers along the King's Highway was the Seth Spring Tavern and House on Spring's Island. Spring's Island divides the Saco River into two main channels. The river was used for its power, and around 1775, mills and dams were built on it. The river itself falls forty-seven feet, perfect as a source of power. The land on the island was purchased around 1704 by Seth Spring, a veteran of the Battle of Bunker Hill in the Revolutionary War. He constructed a bridge to the Biddeford mainland and then built another to Saco at approximately the same locations where today's bridges are located.

In 1798, Spring built a house and tavern on the island that was located on the King's Highway. This highway was also called the Boston to Portland Road, and the house and tavern was a very popular stop for stagecoaches traveling along this route. Seth Spring was a very prominent business owner and entrepreneur in the towns and often entertained notable people from the area and those traveling from Boston and Portland, including General Lafayette, who was a guest there in 1825.

Around 1900, this fine building was converted to a tenement house. Recently, the Seth Spring house and tavern on Elm Street in Biddeford has been enjoying a new life as the office building for the Deering Lumber Company.

Seth Spring Tavern, Biddeford. *Author photo.*

THE CHASE TAVERN, BUXTON (1815–PRESENT)

The Chase Tavern, located at 3 Old Orchard Road in Buxton, was built around the turn of the nineteenth century by Benjamin Toppin Chase. After Chase married Submit Woodman in 1815, they opened a store and tavern. It became a stop for travelers on the stagecoach line between New Hampshire and Portland. They also provided supplies for the stagecoaches.

In the early 1870s, the house became the headquarters for the Buxton and Hollis Agricultural Society's annual fairs, which were held in the nearby park. The ballroom and dining area in the house were used to entertain fairgoers.

In 1908, the property was purchased by A.L.T. Cummings, city clerk of Portland, as a summer home. He renovated the home and renamed it Crossways. The house was used to entertain the political and social elite from Portland and Buxton. The home was purchased by Ronald H.R. Smith in 2000, renovated and became the Buxton Professional Center and the home office of RHR Smith & Company, Certified Public Accountants. Many of the original features of the house were retained.

Rufus Porter mural, Chase Tavern, Buxton. *Author photo.*

This historic house revealed a surprise after renovations began in the early 2000s. After seven layers of wallpaper were removed from what is now the conference room, a beautiful mural was uncovered that was painted in the early 1830s by the famous artist Rufus Porter. Porter was best known for his murals, which span New England, and was also the founder of the *Scientific American* magazine, the oldest continuously published monthly magazine in the United States. The room was evaluated and the mural fully restored thanks to the Buxton Historic Society. The tavern is listed in the National Register of Historic Places.

The Starbird Tavern, East Fairfield (1836–Present)

The Starbird Tavern, later called Willow-Wood, was established in 1836 in East Fairfield by Silas Starbird. The tavern was originally two stories high. It had a bar in the southeast corner and a dance hall on the second floor. It was a favorite overnight stop between Augusta and Norridgewock. At the age of ninety, Joseph Nye, who lived nearby, recalled it as a frequent stop after log drives on the Kennebec and the site of gay events.

John Starbird, father of Silas, managed the tavern for many years and lived there with his wife, Mary (Bates); they raised their five children there until his death in 1846. Mary continued to operate the tavern until her own death ten years later, when it was taken over by her son Silas. Silas Bates Starbird married Adelaide, daughter of Thomas Totman, postmaster of East Fairfield, in 1856, and they were the parents of nine children—all of whom were born in the Starbird Tavern. These children were raised in the tavern as a home. For many years, Silas Starbird prospered. In fact, as a young man he was able to hire a substitute to fight in his place during the Civil War. He was a farmer in addition to an innkeeper. He also had a large business in sheep. He raised, purchased and sold sheep, as well as being involved in the wool-making industry. His barn was one hundred feet long and intended for both sheep raising and wool storage. He was a selectman of the town in the years 1872–76 and may have served as postmaster in East Fairfield. But he suffered financial losses, and in 1878, the Starbirds moved to California. In 1881, the bank took over the property, and the tavern remained closed for several years.

WILLIAM EVERETT'S TAVERN, ELIOT (1649–1690)

One of the earliest taverns in the District of Maine was William Everett's Tavern in Eliot. Near what was known as Joselyn Point and later Leighton's Point, sea captain William Everett built a large three-story house in about 1640 and was licensed to keep a tavern in 1649. An important event in Maine's history took place at this tavern. It was at Everett's Tavern that the Court of General Sessions and other town meetings were held. On November 16, 1652, the residents of Kittery signed the Submission to Massachusetts, with William Everett being the last to put his name to the document. The Submission to Massachusetts was a proposal to keep the District of Maine as part of Massachusetts. The first settlers of Maine, unlike those of Massachusetts who came for religious freedom, came to fish. They were not particularly interested in allowing any one form of religion to dominate. Very often, business came before religion. Massachusetts was afraid this freedom of thought would interfere with the government they wanted to establish in New England. So, a survey was made, and the people here in Maine were, shall we say, invited to come under the Massachusetts government. The commissioners came up from Boston to Kittery but did not meet with success. Then another commission was sent with a stronger message that Massachusetts had "just right and jurisdiction over the land" and "required" their submission. They added that the inhabitants were required to gather at the Tavern of William Everett to "settle the government amongst you." After quite an emotionally heated day, in November 1652, the document was finally signed by forty men and one woman (Mary Beadle Bachiler), and thus they acknowledged themselves subject to Massachusetts. Kittery became a new shire, or what is now known as a county seat of government.

William Everett lost his life at sea soon after, and his widow and her new husband sold this historic building to Captain William Leighton in 1656. William's son John Leighton inherited the property from his father and eventually took the house down and, in 1690, built somewhat east of here what was known as the Old Leighton House. The highway at that time ran to the northeast of the present River Road and behind the Old Parish Burial Ground, just ahead. There is a plaque at the site where the tavern once stood.

Everett Tavern plaque, Eliot. *Author photo.*

One other point of interest: Stackpole, writing in *Old Kittery and Her Families*, did not agree that Everett's Tavern sat at the spot where the plaque has been placed. The plaque is located at 248 River Road in Kittery. He believed the building sat near the water along the road to Watts Fort and that the site has since washed away, along with the rest of the land on the point. Wherever the location may have been takes nothing away from the historic significance of what took place at Everett's Tavern in 1652. This tavern is a great example of how taverns were used for local gatherings as, in this case, holding this important town meeting.

TAVERNS TO INNS TO HOTELS

Most of the first taverns in Maine were just that—simply taverns. Some had accommodations for overnight stay, but most were public houses where local citizens could congregate for drink and entertainment and where they met to hold meetings and decide how their towns were to be run.

Settlers began to reach out to conduct businesses in nearby towns, and as they did, there was more of a demand for them to stay more than one night, so these taverns evolved into more elaborate inns. The biggest expansion came when stagecoaches were replaced by railroads and people started to travel longer distances to conduct business and for pleasure, too. The first passenger railroad in Maine was the Bangor and Piscataquis Canal and Railroad, which traveled about twelve miles from Bangor through Veazie and Old Town to Milford. This railroad eventually joined with the Bangor and Katahdin Railroad in 1891 to become the Bangor and Aroostook Railroad. Farther south, railroads were beginning to connect Maine with the rest of New England, as well, and in 1840, the Boston and Maine Railroad, made up of the existing Andover and Wilmington Railroad and the Boston and Lowell Railroad in Massachusetts, began building a railroad north to Portland. This expansion now meant that those living and working in Maine could travel by rail between Portland, Maine, and Boston, Massachusetts. This was key to the expansion of business and why the earlier taverns and inns finally were replaced by more elaborate hotels where people could stay for extended periods.

The following are a few of the taverns, inns and hotels worth mentioning. By the early to mid-1800s, there were more than three hundred taverns, inns and hotels operating in Maine. The expansion began in earnest in southern and coastal Maine, where most of Maine's residents lived, but eventually migrated through interior Maine all the way north, east and west to the Canadian border.

Eliot

Benjamin Kennard's Tavern in Eliot was built in 1790 by Dr. James H. Pierpoint. Kennard, who was a baker and tavern keeper, purchased the property in 1801. He had a swing sign suspended on one of the large elms out front.

Kennard dealt mainly in West India goods, primarily rum, molasses, tobacco, pipes, snuff and salt fish. Eliot town meetings were held here. His eldest son, William Leighton Kennard, took over the tavern business. In the late 1890s, Dr. John Willis bought the property with the thought of having a sanitarium. He deemed it one of the most beautiful spots in this part of town. It was later the home of Fred K. Nelson and today is owned by Larry McCullough as Pine Tree Farm, a retreat and arts workshop center. This is a good example of an early tavern in Maine where town meetings were held.

Wells

The **Littlefield Tavern** on the Chase L. Charles Road in Wells was built about 1735 by Captain James Littlefield, a slave owner, and operated by Francis Littlefield Sr., the eldest son of Edmund Littlefield, commonly referred to as the "Father of Wells." While an accepted custom in the colonies, slavery was also practiced in Maine as early as 1660, and in 1733, the parish at York (then Agamenticus) "VOTED that there be a slave bought for the Parish to be Employed for the use of said Parish in Labouring for the Rev. Samuel Moody." In 1736, a female African American slave was obtained for Moody. A slave cemetery is located across the street from the tavern.

Kennebunk

One of the first inns to be built in Maine was the **Waldo Emerson Inn** in Kennebunk. It was built by Waldo Emerson in 1753. He was the great-uncle to Ralph Waldo Emerson, who is rumored to have spent ten summers at the house. The house was later inherited through marriage by Theodore Lyman, who added the enormous addition in 1784 as a wedding gift for his wife. Former owners made a fortune as shipbuilders on the Kennebunk River behind the house, so elaborate houses were within their means. George Bourne, a former resident, built the famous Wedding Cake house next door for his second wife. The Waldo Emerson Inn was allegedly also a stop along the Underground Railroad.

This historic home includes a keeping room, a room directly off the kitchen typical in colonial-era homes. In addition, the inn has two spacious parlors. The house boasts several unique architectural features, such as hand-painted Wedgewood tiles adorning the parlor fireplace, Indian shutters and exposed beams dating back to the early 1600s. All the guest rooms are charmingly decorated with attention to comfort and details, including fireplaces in four of the rooms.

West Baldwin

The **Burnell Tavern** in West Baldwin was built in 1737 by Gideon Burnell and is the oldest building in the community and a local landmark.

The tavern is on the principal route between the coast of southern Maine and Fryeburg, which was the location of the Native American community known as Pequawket. Burnell also operated a local gristmill, sawmills and a store. The tavern catered to travelers traveling between Portland and central New Hampshire.

The Burnell tavern served as a stagecoach stop, and the original barn with intact horse and oxen stalls remain. One of Burnell's sons served as the station master when the railroad came through the town. The stagecoach and railway met at this junction. You can still see the abandoned railroad tracks where the rolling pastures of the current property meet the timber acres and see the dirt roadway leading to the Saco River. In one of the front parlors of the present home, you can see cabinets that remain from when it was the town post office. The town general store was moved to

Burnell Tavern. *Collections of Baldwin Historical Society, MHS 18236.*

the property on the right side of the driveway leading to the house. The original plaster walls and wood stove remain in the house.

This house/tavern was professionally restored. It was listed in the National Register of Historic Places on December 29, 1983.

Hiram

The **Mount Cutler House** in Hiram was built in 1846 by J.P. Hubbard. The thirty-two-room inn/tavern was a favorite stop for travelers on the Conway, New Hampshire, to Portland stagecoach along the Pequawket Trail. The buildings were razed in 1968.

The house was the residence of Thomas Libby. Later, it was cut in two sections and part of it moved. The portion that was moved became the V.T. Shaw's store and remained a seasonal store until 2012. A stagecoach from the Mount Cutler House was used in the play *Rebecca of Sunnybrook Farm*.

North Newry

The **Poplar Tavern** was built about 1854 by Ithiel Smith and originally named the Popple Tree House. This tavern is an excellent example of a hostelry that started as a tavern and evolved into a hotel in later years. Charles Bartlett purchased the tavern from Smith and changed the name to the Poplar Hotel. He operated the tavern for twenty-six years before moving away.

Sometime during the 1880s, a group of old guests got together and purchased the property, and it was known as the Bear River Club House. In 1892, Scott A. Godwin was managing the house. In 1895, a Mr. Kilgore was manager, and additions were made at this time, including billiard and pool tables. In 1898, when first-class board was $2.25 per week, the old office and reception room were torn down and rebuilt. A year later, the property was advertised for rent as being able to accommodate sixty-five guests, including tennis courts, a billiard hall and a livery stable. In 1900, Mr. and Mrs. Coburn of Bethel were running the hotel. By 1901, W.W. (Wallace) Kilgore was operating the hotel, which was transferred to him by the Bear River Club. Wallace would change the name to Poplar Tavern, and it was he who constructed cabins or cottages to supplement the hotel itself. Under his management, the price rose to $12 per week.

By 1903, Kilgore had built some cabins on the property and built a store onto the hotel. The hotel featured a piazza, one of the first taverns to have one. Kilgore's brother Dennis ran the tavern, cabins and store beginning in 1911, when Wallace moved to Bethel to open a similar business there. During those years, Poplar Tavern was basically a summer business. Wallace sold the business to James and Inez Martin, but he regained ownership in 1939–40 and sold it again to Sam Smith, who changed the name yet again, this time to the Appalachian House. During his years of ownership, Smith built an annex onto the tavern known locally as the Club House.

Augusta

Augusta had several taverns in the 1700s and 1800s. **Thomas's Tavern** was built in 1784 at the corner of Grove and Green Streets. David Thomas opened another tavern near Fort Western. Amos Pollard built **Pollard's Tavern** in 1784 on Market Square, and it was in this Augusta tavern that frequent public meetings were held. **Whitney's Tavern** was built in the late 1700s and was located at the corner of Bangor and Clark Streets. **Reed's Tavern**, another popular tavern, was built down from Whitney's Tavern on Bangor Street.

Hallowell

The town of Hallowell was considered the center for trade on the Kennebec River in the 1700s and 1800s. In addition to the Hallowell House mentioned earlier, **Currier's Tavern** was located on Water Street and was frequented by sailors and others in the shipping trade. **Norris's Tavern** on the Old Hallowell Road was built in the early 1800s and frequented by travelers west of there going to and from Hallowell. Another very popular tavern was **Piper's Tavern** on Water Street.

Litchfield

Bachelder's Tavern was a popular tavern in Litchfield located at the crossroads known through the years as South Litchfield. The tavern was built in 1818 by Asa Bachelder of brick manufactured right on the property. It became a stagecoach stop on the Augusta to Portland route. Horses and buggies were put up there while the stagecoach drivers ate and stayed at the tavern. Many public meetings and trials by circuit court judges were held there. This tavern is a good example of one catering to those traveling by stagecoach and where circuit judges held court.

Bangor

The **Bangor House Hotel** was built in 1833–34 by a group of Bangor businessmen seeking to create a luxurious accommodation like the famous Tremont House in Boston, which was considered one of the finest hotels in the United States. It is a four-story building on the corner of Union and Main Streets. Originally built in a U shape open to the south, the inside of the U was filled in with a billiard hall, and wings were added to the east and south in 1869. It cost $125,000 to build and furnish, which was a significant amount of money in the mid-1800s. The tavern area of the hotel was reportedly one of the most frequented in the Bangor area. Much of the contents of the tavern area was copied from earlier taverns in Massachusetts.

The hotel was designed by famous architect Charles Bryant and was considered one of the nation's greatest luxurious hotels for more than a century. Guests who stayed at the Bangor House included Presidents Theodore Roosevelt, Ulysses S. Grant, William Howard Taft, Arthur McKinley and Benjamin Harrison. The hotel also accommodated John Philip Sousa, Gene Autry, Jack Benny, Rudy Vallee, Bette Davis, Duke Ellington, Henry Fonda, Tommy Dorsey, Ted Williams, Liberace, Amelia Earhart and other famous people. The hotel was, indeed, before its time. It had its own water supply from water tanks on the roof, and each room had a fireplace and steam heat, unheard of at the time. Elevators were added at the end of the 1800s.

A murder occurred at the Bangor House in 1865 that remains unsolved. A fifty-four-year-old chambermaid was found by a co-worker in a vacant third-floor room after being missing for two days. She had been raped and strangled to death. Some at the time thought the Boston Strangler might have been the killer because of similarities to those murdered in Boston. Massachusetts authorities came to Bangor to follow up but concluded that enough discrepancies existed to rule that out.

Bangor endured the Great Fire of 1911, which destroyed much of the city's downtown area, but the Bangor House escaped, reportedly because it was on its own block and not connected to other buildings. But it had to survive its own fire on Christmas morning in 1954, when the entire west wing of the hotel was completely gutted. Seventy-one guests were forced to flee outside in fifteen-degree weather in only their nightclothes. Firefighters from Bangor, Brewer and Dow Air Force Base responded to the fire. Six firefighters suffered injuries fighting the blaze. The fire destroyed twenty rooms on the Summer Street side of the building in the back of the hotel. This wing had to be razed and rebuilt.

As Bangor expanded to having shopping malls outside the city, business downtown fell off dramatically, and the Bangor House started to lose significant business. The hotel was purchased by Abraham Shapiro in 1973, and he, in turn, sold the building to State Street Management Co., which converted the building into low-income elderly housing. It still serves this purpose today, with 120 senior apartments. The hotel was listed in the National Register of Historic Places in 1972.

The **PENOBSCOT EXCHANGE HOTEL** on Exchange Street in Bangor was built in 1827 and remodeled a number of times. Its proximity to Eastern Railway station was an advantage to travelers. It was built in 1827 by Zadok French. The hotel had 150 rooms and was one of the first in Maine to have both an elevator and a garage. It was known locally as French's Folley. In 1828, the Penobscot Exchange Coffee House, named after Boston's Exchange Coffee House, opened in the hotel. It originally consisted of a brick building with four and a half stories, a gabled roof and eight chimneys, but in 1908, a city ordinance required all downtown buildings to have flat roofs to alleviate danger from ice and snow. So, the building was expanded at that time to add a fifth floor, and modern bathrooms were added at that time. In the mid-twentieth century, the building was briefly a dormitory for Husson College, but it was eventually razed in the Urban Renewal program of the 1960s.

HOULTON

The **SNELL HOUSE** was Houlton's premier hotel at the end of the nineteenth century. Its owners also owned Central Stables, which was a huge draw, as travelers could have their horses put up next to where they were staying and have any repairs needed to team harnesses or carriages done there as well. The hotel was located at Market Square in Houlton. The first automobile to visit Houlton was driven to the hotel by Deputy Sheriff Patrick Cassidy in 1900. An advertisement in the *Houlton Times* appearing on April 2, 1919, states, "Situated in Houlton, the very heart of the world famous Aroostook County, Maine. The hotel will accommodate 100 guests—not a dark room or courtroom in the house. Every room opens to the sunlight, this very few hotels in the United States can say. A Sunday home for the commercial traveler and tourist."

The **EXCHANGE HOTEL** came into existence in 1872 when William D. Buzzell, who came to Houlton in 1845, decided to open a business on Main Street and soon decided to operate a hotel. This was his first venture in the hotel business. He renovated his home into a hotel, known as the Buzzell Hotel, in 1872. It was managed by Charles H. Sleeper for the first year or two. In 1874–75, it became known as the Exchange Hotel. This building, along with all its contents, was lost in the fire of 1880. Buzzell purchased a lot on Court Street and rebuilt at once a four-story building with sixty-two rooms. It was well known and a favorite of businessmen and county officials. When the foundation for the building was laid in 1880, bystanders, who always know best, warned Buzzell that he could not expect to fill all the rooms as planned. Within one year, Buzzell had added an addition for ten more rooms. The building was lost to fire in 1942 and not rebuilt.

Clark's Hotel started as a large boarding home on Kendall Street by James N. Clark after the Civil War in 1865. It was renamed the Farmers Hotel in 1882 and Clark's Hotel in 1883. Clients noted that the building was "meticulously kept and capably operated." It was frequented often by lumber and railroad promoters, and allegedly, many financial deals were negotiated there.

Presque Isle

The **Reed Tavern**, founded by Leonard Reed in 1842, was the third building in the village of Presque Isle and the first hostelry (lodging) built on the land where the **Northeastland Hotel** is today. In 1884, a devastating fire broke out and burned the tavern, which also served as a hotel, to the ground. Another hotel, the **Presque Isle House Hotel**, was built on the same location. In January 1900, the Presque Isle House Hotel was destroyed by fire. The remnants of the building were not demolished until September 1930 in getting ready for the construction of a new hotel, the Northeastland, on the same site. The Northeastland Hotel is still thriving.

Scarborough

Ira Foss built the **Checkley House Hotel** in the 1870s at the tip of Prouts Neck in Scarborough, later known as Checkley Point. The hotel was named after Samuel Checkley, one of the early settlers of Scarborough. The building started as a boardinghouse, expanding several times over the years until Foss's death in 1919. His widow ran the hotel after his death. Mr. Foss was an innovative hotel owner. The water system he built for the hotel also benefited the neighboring homes. He purchased electrical generators for the hotel to provide power for his pumps and elevators and lighting before electricity was readily available. He supplied horse-drawn wagons to meet every train at the Scarborough station to transport people to the Neck. The Foss family sold the hotel in the early 1940s. It was razed in 1944 after five years of blackouts and coastal evacuations caused by World War II.

The **ATLANTIC HOUSE** came into being in 1855, when Enoch Nutter rented out rooms in his farmhouse at Scarborough Beach. Additions were built in 1877 and 1911, and a portion of the hotel was torn down around 1911–12. For many years, cattle could be seen grazing on the front lawn of the Atlantic House because it was still a working farm.

In 1923, Joseph Knight became the owner of the hotel and promptly modernized and redecorated it. He had local artist Roger Deering paint murals for the lobby. These murals are now on display at the Scarborough Historical Society. Joseph Knight's son Harry ran the hotel after his father's retirement until his early death. The hotel was sold and continued operating until 1988, when it was torn down.

BELFAST

The **WINDSOR HOTEL** on High Street was a centerpiece of Belfast for over one hundred years, outlasting several downtown hotels. It was originally the New England House, opened in 1848 by Luther Coombs in a dwelling. "No pains or expenditures will be spared in repairing and furnishing the house, erecting outbuildings and fitting them up in a style best calculated to promote the comfort and happiness of the traveling public," he declared. He conducted his business on strictly temperance principles. The name was changed to the Windsor Hotel in 1885, and the adjacent tenement building became the hotel annex as business grew. A horse-drawn coach met guests at the steamship wharf. Benjamin Harrison, Theodore Roosevelt, William Howard Taft and Warren G. Harding were among the hotel's famous guests.

ROCKLAND

The **BAY POINT HOTEL**, owned by Francis Cobb II, opened on July 4, 1889. In 1902, the Ricker family, owners and operators of the Poland Spring Hotel, bought the property and embellished the L-shaped building with turrets, porches and gingerbread decoration. Hiram Ricker renamed the hotel the Samoset, after the Pemaquid chief who was among the first people to greet Europeans. In 1911, the Maine Central Railroad acquired the hotel. The hotel closed in 1969 and burned completely on October 13, 1972. A new Samoset was built in 1978 and is a successful and extremely popular hotel to this day.

CASTINE

The **AVERY HOUSE**, the oldest house still standing in Castine, was built in the 1760s. It was known as Yellow Ball Tavern when Castine was the shire town of Hancock County (1796–1838). It was probably the first "drive through" tavern in the United States. Horsemen riding to the courthouse on Castine Common could order a mug of rum or beer without dismounting; they simply rode up to one side of the ell, paid for their drink and rode out the other side! The Muster of Troops was held on the Military Muster Grounds on the Avery House property. Soldiers were very often accompanied by their families and camped out on the property, allowing them to attend entertainments, like peep shows and dances, in the ell of the tavern. This is clearly one of the most historic buildings in historic Castine.

PORTLAND

In September 1681, the selectmen of Casco lobbied and were granted by the court a license allowing Richard Seacomb to keep an ordinary, or tavern, in Portland near India Street. This license is believed to be the first of its kind granted in the area. Richard Seacomb, Portland's first known hotelier, came from England to America in 1660 and fathered three children. He served as a selectman and in 1684 was made constable. Seacomb died in 1694. In addition to providing lodging for travelers, **SEACOMB'S TAVERN** offered patrons meals and liquor. In May 1682, Seacomb was fined fifty shillings after it was discovered that he had sold liquor to American Indians, which was against the law.

As the city grew, more travelers began arriving via different means of transportation. In 1818, the first passenger coach line from Portland to

Boston opened, and by 1832, twelve stagecoach lines ran through the city, with five coaches arriving and departing daily. To capitalize on this constant stream of travelers, three hotels in particular—the American, Cumberland and the Elm—went up near Portland City Hall where the stagecoaches stopped to let off and take on passengers. These three hotels mark the beginning of the lively Portland hotel business and the growth of the city itself.

The **AMERICAN HOUSE** at the corner of Fore and Lime Streets prided itself on offering travelers a convenient place to stay in the "business part of the city." While the American House's more modest furnishings paled in the face of its competitor and neighbor, the Cumberland House, the hotel still presented "great inducements for travelers."

In the mid-1830s, the newly built **CUMBERLAND HOUSE** was considered to be a "truly magnificent hotel." Located at the junction of Middle, Main, Federal, Congress and Elm Streets (Monument Square, formerly Haymarket Square), the Cumberland House advertised "parlors and meals at any hour." The hotel's proximity to both the eastern and western stagecoach lines made it a convenient stopping place for travelers passing through the area. When it first opened, the hotel boasted eighteen parlors and fifty-seven bedrooms. Accommodations for men were offered in the Eastern Wing, while the "tastefully prepared" rooms of the West Wing were reserved for women and families. In addition to the hotel's well-appointed rooms and exquisite furnishings—all of which cost the hotel a total of $15,000—the Cumberland was also the site of an acclaimed restaurant frequented by hotel guests and locals.

On December 13, 1825, the *Eastern Argus* newspaper advertised the opening of the **ELM TAVERN** with Thomas S. Bowles, proprietor. The advertisement featured a woodcut of a stagecoach parked in front of a handsome brick building, shaded by a large elm tree from which the hotel took its name. The stagecoach in the woodcut was a nod to the hotel's intention to serve travelers coming into Portland along the recently opened stage lines. Thomas S. Bowles kept the hotel for only three years, when he was succeeded by John Appleton, a future state representative for the district. As landlord, Appleton saw the Elm become the headquarters of every stage line that ran through the city, a significant advantage for a hotel catering to stagecoach travelers. The Elm continued to offer accommodations to these and other travelers until Portland's Great Fire of 1866. After the fire, the Elm was rebuilt and went on to become the headquarters of Kendall and Whitney, a distributor of agricultural machinery.

An early 1900s advertisement pamphlet for the **COLUMBIA HOTEL** lauds it as an "unusual combination of comfort, convenience, and economy." The Columbia Hotel at 645A Congress Street was built in 1895 and later housed the studios of WGAN television. It is thought that the hotel was named in remembrance of the World's Columbian Exposition. The hotels rooms were "cheerful, large and with plenty of windows and fine beds." The hotel also advertised affordable dining, with individual breakfasts as low as twenty-five cents and catering for large gatherings. The Columbia was also well known in the city for its Hawaiian Room, a cocktail lounge offering "intimate entertainment for your enjoyment." However, in the early 1960s, the hotel began experiencing economic troubles and was foreclosed in May 1961. After investing almost $1 million in the structure, a group of prominent businessmen opened the new Portlander In-Town Motel, ushering in a new chapter in the history of the building.

Since its construction in 1927, the **EASTLAND** has held the position as Portland's most prominent hotel. Built at the expense of $2 million and designed by local architect Herbert Rhodes, it was the largest building in Portland for many years. The Eastland's colorful history began with a pompous opening ceremony that included Graham McNamee, a well-known radio personality of the time, dropping the keys to the new hotel into Portland Harbor from an airplane—an act to signify that the hotel would never close. Around five thousand individuals toured the hotel at the opening reception, and a select group of local elite was treated to a meal in the Spanish Baronial dining room. Around the time of its opening, the Eastland advertised "369 rooms and 369 baths," as well as 140 other apartments and shops. Throughout the latter half of the twentieth century, the Eastland began a turbulent chapter in its history. In the early 1960s, the Eastland and the adjacent Congress Square Hotel were sold to a New Hampshire firm, Dunfey Corporation, for a sum of $2.5 million. It renamed the hotel the Sheraton-Eastland Motor Hotel. In the early 1970s, the hotel changed hands again as Aetna Life of Hartford, Connecticut, purchased the property.

In 1981, a three-alarm fire raged through the hotel's ballroom, forcing residents to evacuate. Later, in 1983, Sonesta International Hotel Corporation obtained the hotel, stating that "professional hotel people" were needed to keep the hotel afloat. Sonesta put the hotel through a $5 million renovation, only to sell it in 1992 to Innkeepers Ltd. of Pennsylvania for $3.5 million. Five years later, the Eastland was sold once again, this time to a Florida company for $9 million. In 2013, the Eastland again changed hands, and it is now the Westin Portland Harborview Hotel.

Beginning with lively opening day celebrations in 1868, the **Falmouth Hotel** developed a reputation of grandeur and excellence. Charles Alexander, a New York architect, designed the hotel's stately six-story structure at 212 Middle Street for John B. Brown shortly after Portland's Great Fire of 1866. The grand two-hundred-room hotel with its wide corridors, marble fireplaces and high ceilings quickly became a Portland landmark. Costing a total of $300,000 to construct and furnish, the hotel was dubbed "the most luxurious hotel this side of New York" by a local newspaper. In its day, the hotel was a significant political and social center, noted for hosting numerous banquets that earned it the nickname "hotel of a million banquets." Presidents Grant, McKinley, Theodore Roosevelt, Taft and Harding all stayed at the Falmouth over the years. In 1898, the hotel entertained General William Tecumseh Sherman, along with a slew of other famous officers of the time. For many years, the hotel was the headquarters for the Maine Republican Party. After a remarkable ninety years of operating, the Falmouth turned off its lights and closed its doors in early November 1958. The hotel was deemed a fire hazard and was torn down to make way for a parking lot in 1963, just five years before it would have celebrated its 100th anniversary.

Built on the site of the former Mussey Boarding House where General Lafayette supposedly stayed during a visit to Portland in 1825, the grand **Lafayette Hotel** opened its doors in 1903. The hotel, located at 638 Congress Street, boasted 250 rooms—all of which offered hot and cold water. Daily rates at the hotel ranged from $2.50 to $7.00. The hotel offered meals in the Crystal Room, a beauty shop, a barbershop and the Lafayette Lounge, where a large painting depicting the surrender of Cornwallis hung on the wall. The Lafayette hosted many conventions, including the Maine Democratic Convention, a gathering of some 2,500 individuals from around the state. In 1971, the Lafayette abandoned the hotel format and turned many of its rooms into apartments. Around this same time, the Lafayette began to slide into disrepair. However, the hotel underwent major renovations in the mid-1990s and is still standing.

Situated on the southern coast of Peaks Island, the **Peaks Island House** advertised itself as a retreat for those seeking the pleasures of the Casco Bay Islands. The hotel itself was just "30 rodes from the ocean" and offered fine views of Casco Bay. The hotel boasted a variety of facilities for "fishing, sea bathing and water excursions." In the late 1850s, the steamer *Gipsey* sailed from the island to Portland three times a day.

Once the home of Commodore Edward Preble—the man sometimes considered to be the father of the American navy—the **Preble House** was, at one time, the second-largest hotel in Portland, surpassed only by the Falmouth. Commodore Edward Preble oversaw the building's construction in 1806, but he never lived in the house, as he died before the home could be completely furnished. However, his wife and son did take up residence in the stately mansion. The rooms in the mansion were large and fashionably furnished. The Preble House was noted as the first building in Portland, and possibly the state, to heat using a furnace rather than wood stoves. After the death of the commodore's wife in 1851, the mansion was transformed into a hotel and opened its doors on March 19, 1860. The hotel rose four stories and was fronted on the Congress Street side by several tall elms. The hotel offered 150 rooms "furnished in the most modern style" and was considered by some to be one of the finest hotels in America. In the summer of 1860, Stephen Douglas, Democratic candidate for president, visited the hotel and delivered a speech to a crowd from the hotel's balcony. Around this same time, the Prince of Wales, who would later become King Edward VII, visited the city and was given an impressive reception at the hotel. Several stores occupied the ground floor of the hotel, including C.W. Robinson & Co. Dry Goods. The hotel closed and was torn down in 1923 to make way for the new twelve-story Chapman Building.

Standing on Haymarket (later Monument) Square at the corner of Federal and Market Streets in Portland, the **UNITED STATES HOTEL** held the moniker of one of the oldest hotels in Portland for many years. The United States Hotel stood five stories tall and offered 150 rooms. In 1874–75, the hotel underwent extensive renovations "which at once stamped it as a superior class hotel." With these renovations came telegraph services for guests, a reading room, a billiard room and additional bathrooms. The United States Hotel became a popular spot for those traveling for pleasure and business alike. In 1855, former president Millard Fillmore visited Portland and "took lodgings at the United States Hotel," reported the *Portland Inquirer*. The well-known actor Bill Hickock also stayed at the hotel. In 1900, the United States Hotel closed its doors, and the firm Edwards and Walker began operating out of the building.

ARE SOME HISTORIC MAINE TAVERNS AND INNS HAUNTED?

There are many stories that abound about strange occurrences that happened in Maine taverns and inns. Here are a few stories of eerie happenings over the years.

Durham

The **Royalsborough Inn at Bagley House** at 1290 Royalsborough Road was built in 1772. Guests staying there throughout the years tell stories of hearing whispers of the ghost of a former maid, and some male guests have reported being touched by unseen hands.

Freeport

The **Jameson Tavern** referred to earlier in the book not only is allegedly the Birthplace of Maine but may be inhabited by a resident ghost, as well. The ghost of a little girl named Emily is frequently seen by guests staying there. She used to live in part of what is now the attic of the tavern. She shows herself to elders and also plays with children visiting there. Some believe she simply does not realize she has died.

Bar Harbor

The **Coach Stop Inn** located at 715 State Highway 3 is a former tavern and coach stop in Bar Harbor. It is home to Abbe, a spirited little girl who loves music. Strange noises, flickering lights and fleeting reflections of Abbe often appear.

Kennebunkport

The **Captain Fairfield Inn** is a Federal-style mansion built in 1813 for Captain James Fairfield after he had been released from British imprisonment during the War of 1812. It was a wedding present presented to Fairfield and his bride, Lois, from his father-in-law. Captain Fairfield lived in the home for five years until he died of pneumonia. He liked it so much he may have never left! It was converted to an inn in 1991, and reports of hauntings have come in ever since. Guests report feeling the warm presence of an image of the captain who seems very pleased to have so many people enjoying his home. One story told depicts seeing an image of the captain in the basement during renovation to turn the home into an inn.

What is now known as the **Tides Beach Club** at 254 Kings Highway at Goose Rocks Beach had its beginning as the Tides Inn By-the-Sea. It was built in 1899 by Emma Foss, and it is her ghost that is rumored to still haunt the inn and let several owners over the years know that she did not like the changes they had made.

Rockland

The **Captain Lindsey House**, located at 5 Lindsey Street, was first built in 1837 and was one of Rockland's first inns. The inn has been renovated over the years and now looks very much like it did when it was owned by Captain Lindsey. So many incidents of paranormal activity have been reported that it can claim to be one of the most haunted inns in Maine. There have been people staying on the first floor who report they have heard people and furniture moving around upstairs when no one else is in the building. Others have heard voices, and some have even stated they saw a woman's face in a sitting room cabinet. Beds that were neatly made have had mysterious handprints or seat impressions appear when no one has been in the room.

Bethel

One of the oldest buildings in Bethel is the **Chapman Inn** at 2 Church Street. It was built by a retired sea captain in 1865, and shortly after, the inn was purchased by William Rogers Chapman. The inn design has never been altered from the original floorplan. But it appears that at least two of the residents—Chapman's daughter Abigail and her nanny—never left. Professional paranormal investigators confirm the stories of hauntings. Abigail was a sickly child who spent most of her time indoors. This led to William Chapman hiring a nanny to provide her companionship and additional help. After Abigail died, her nanny remained in the home. Visitors have experienced cold drafts in unopened rooms even during the hot summer months and also report doors opening and closing without assistance. They also report hearing footsteps when no one is around and have heard a young woman's voice coming from empty rooms. But the most bizarre happening is seeing a black cat leaving a room when people enter and seeing the cat walk through solid walls. All of these happenings certainly lead to the belief that the Chapman Inn is one of the most haunted inns in Maine.

Rockland

The **LimeRock Inn** was built as a private residence in 1892 at 96 Limerock Street. In 1950, the house became the private residence and medical office for Dr. Oren Lawry Jr. Many of the ghosts that linger in the LimeRock Inn today are believed to be Dr. Lawry's former patients. People report they have spotted what appears to be his patients in the stairwell of the inn, while others have been seen in the parlor and foyer. Some people report hearing sounds of hushed talking in the parlor area and seeing the ghosts of two little girls. Paranormal experts visiting the inn state they have felt the presence of many people in the front parlor, which was the area Dr. Lawry used as his waiting room.

Greenville

The **Greenville Inn** at 40 Norris Street was built around 1890 by William Shaw about a decade before he became a wealthy lumber baron. The inn has had multiple owners over the years, and all of them strived to keep it in its original state. It is believed that a young woman is a permanent resident, although long since passed. Some who have seen and interacted with her claim she is a very sweet and friendly woman.

Poland Springs

In 1876, Hiram Ricker opened the **Poland Spring House**, which shortly became a popular attraction for the country's social and political elite. The hotel was eventually composed of over 350 guest rooms, a barbershop, dance and photography studios, a pool room, a music hall, a bowling alley and dining facilities. The inn is believed to be haunted by Hiram Ricker himself. Employees report seeing him walking around and hearing his voice when in empty rooms. In the empty lobby, employees report hearing footsteps in the early morning hours and notice objects in the lobby have been moved to different places. The reports of ghostly activity are not confined to the inn itself. At least two reported ghosts were picked up while hitchhiking on nearby Route 26, allegedly a bride who was struck by a car and killed on her way to a wedding and a girl in a prom dress. Reportedly, both of these hitchhikers will accept rides and then disappear unexpectedly either before getting into a car or after.

Dedham

The **Lucerne Inn** at 2517 Main Road dates back to the early 1800s and has been host to numerous reports of paranormal activity. Guests have heard people talking outside when no one is around and report seeing shadows, as well. There are also reports of a murder/suicide whose ghosts still linger there. But there is one room at the inn that has more than its share of paranormal activity. Guests staying in room 8 see shadows on the walls of the room and hear voices outside when no one is there. One guest claimed her door kept opening even after she closed it several times. Inn employees stated the piano at the inn can be heard playing when no one is near it and televisions in rooms, occupied or not, turn on by themselves.

Searsport

The **Carriage House Inn**, Victorian in design, at 120 Main Street (Route 1), was built in 1874 by Captain John McGilvery, one of five brothers who all became ship captains. Both Ernest Hemingway and Waldo Pierce, a famous American painter, reportedly have stayed at the inn. There have been numerous reports of paranormal activity at the inn. It is believed the ghosts of two people who died there unexpectedly remain. And reportedly, the owner's beagle avoided the staircase where a death occurred, as well as rooms where other paranormal activities took place. People claim to have felt someone walk into their room and to smell cigar smoke when nobody is smoking. Others report the sound of knocking, soft whispers and even music playing when no one at the time is playing any music. As an aside, it is interesting to note that in the 1940s, the inn became a garrison for army officers.

Kennebunk

The original building of what is now known as the **Kennebunk Inn** at 45 Main Street was built in 1799 by Phineas Cole. In 1926, the house was purchased from the owners by George Baitler, who converted the home into an inn known as The Tavern, adding a two-and-a-half-story wing to produce thirty guest rooms. The name was changed in the 1930s to the Kennebunk Inn. Ghosts of two former clerks of the inn and one of its previous owners are rumored to still live there. The clerks appear to have had a strong attachment to the inn and, even after their deaths, can be seen performing their duties. Guests and visitors report hearing glasses shake and other unexpected noises, as well.

Falmouth

The **Buckman Tavern** was built in 1776 by Samuel Buckman. The tavern was a popular stagecoach stop on the King's Highway about halfway from Portsmouth, New Hampshire, to Bangor, Maine. The inn is home to alleged tales of terror, including the story of an insane guest who murdered his traveling companion and, as legend has it, tossed the head of his victim out of the top-floor window. Reportedly, every time the pane of broken glass in that particular window is replaced, it cracks shortly thereafter. Another story about the tavern is interesting as well. A deed for the home that was part of the stables on the Buckman Tavern property states that bodies are buried at the bottom of the old well on the property. The well has since been filled in, and a stone outline is all that remains to mark the site.

AMERICA'S TEA STORY

Better to be deprived of food for three days than tea for one.
—Chinese proverb

Tea first arrived from China in the port of London in the middle of the 1600s aboard ships of the East India Company. From there, it spread throughout the world and became the most widely consumed beverage on earth after water. From its first introduction in America by the Dutch in New York City, it quickly became a favorite beverage choice for both men and women. For nearly four centuries, tea has held a remarkable position in our society. It became the symbol of culture and sophistication.

By the 1700s, Boston law, in accordance with English law, required each seller of tea to be licensed. The social customs of early Boston established that when ladies went to social gatherings, each carried her own teacup, saucer and spoon in a bag. The cups were always of the best china, very small and held as much as a common wineglass.

In July 1774, John Adams arrived by horseback at a tavern in Falmouth (now Portland), Maine, as part of his duty as a circuit judge. After a thirty-mile journey, he requested a cup of tea that had been acquired by paying no duty tax. Adams was vehemently opposed to the tax on tea imposed on the colonies by England in the early 1700s. He eased his conscience by drinking only tea smuggled into the country from Holland, which required no taxation.

New Englanders proved to be the most discerning tea drinkers. Their knowledge and use of tea were growing so rapidly that by the late 1700s, nearly half of homes included tea and its paraphernalia. By this time, tea was not only a beverage for breakfast, it was now also a drink in the afternoon. Sugar, honey or molasses was now added to tea, as well as milk or cream by those who could afford it.

Between the 1830s and 1840s, afternoon tea developed into a new social event that was held between lunch at noon and 8:00 p.m. dinner. These "little teas" took place in the afternoon and were so called because of the small amount of food served and the neatness and elegance of the meal. By the end of the century, all classes of people were enjoying their afternoon tea, not just the socially elite. Even in small villages, tea was a more refined occasion. By now, five o'clock tea was recognized as a common social ritual. To present an afternoon tea, you would place your best linen tablecloths on the tea tables, use the best china available and place flowers everywhere. The menu would consist of little sandwiches, cakes, fruits and scones and, of course, a choice of teas—orange Pekoe, Ceylon or Twinings—all delicious! This would be served indoors in the drawing room or, if the weather were really nice, outdoors on the lawn under the shade trees and served on tables

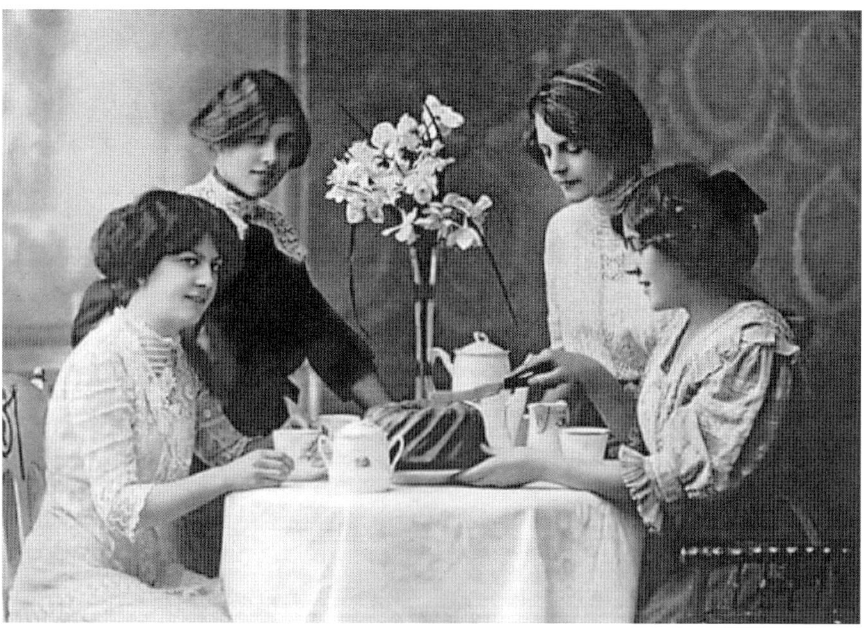

Ladies at tea. *Author collection.*

with white tablecloths, a full tea service and vases of fresh flowers. By the 1880s, there was even a special dress—the tea gown—designed to be worn by genteel ladies to tea.

There is also a high tea. While the afternoon tea consisted mainly of tea, toast and small cakes, a high tea is where meat takes a prominent part and signifies what it really is: a tea dinner. A grand array of sweet and savory dishes would be offered. There would be ripe strawberries with jugs of cream, assorted fruits, cakes of various kinds, gingerbread, hot muffins, toast, scones and tea cakes. The sideboard would hold cold salmon, veal, ham pies, boiled and roasted fowl and roast beef and lamb.

The demand for tea became so popular that commerce was greatly increased. Teas of all kinds, tea services and the accompanying paraphernalia became much in demand, and this, in turn, led to great wealth for some of those involved. Tea drinking brought together goods from all over the world—special tea tables from Britain and the Far East, sweet meats flavored with spices from Indonesia, porcelain from China and sugar from the Caribbean. Some merchants became very wealthy.

Torii Shop and Tea House, Castine (1923)

On the coast of Maine in the town of Castine, Mrs. Grace Knudson and Miss Mable Appleton operated a charming tea house and gift shop. It was located in a warehouse next to a pier and was decorated in true Japanese atmosphere. It was called the Torii, which means "gateway," and was originally started as a venture to entertain friends. Its location next to the pier also attracted many yachters wanting tea and to buy the Oriental fabrics and gifts that were used for décor in the tea house. These two ladies achieved such success buying Oriental imports and serving tea that fifteen years later, their profitable tea room and Asian import business were featured as an inspiration to other women in the popular magazine *Woman's Home Companion*.

A surprising discovery of tea leaves occurred in the late 1700s on the shores of Maine's Casco Bay. An East India ship, the *Grand Turk*, sailing from China to Portland, went aground on Cushing's Point in Cape Elizabeth.

It was loaded with silk cloth and tea from the Orient. This was the largest vessel wrecked in Casco Bay before 1800. For weeks after the shipwreck, the shores of Cape Elizabeth were covered with boxes of silk cloth that had floated to shore and were salvaged and used by the enterprising ladies of the community. And the beaches for weeks thereafter were covered in a new kind of seaweed—tea leaves!

A New York newspaper notice of the day on November 22, 1803, stated: "Auction. The cargo of Mr. John Jacob Astor's ship, the *Beaver*, arrived this past week with 2500 chests of prime teas, produced last season from the best Bohea and Singlo fields; the sale to be conducted by Mr. John Hone, the auctioneer, by open bidding on Mr. Astor's Wharf, foot of Liberty Street." Astor's company shipped furs to Canton, where they were exchanged for Chinese teas that were brought back to New York to be sold at a considerable profit. Born in Germany, Astor immigrated to England as a teenager and worked as a musical instrument manufacturer. He moved to the colonies after the American Revolutionary War, when he entered the fur trade and built a monopoly managing a business empire that extended to the Great Lakes region and Canada and, later, into the American West and Pacific coast. Astor was highly wealthy and became a famed patron of the arts. He was the first multimillionaire in the United States.

Although tea companies were established in Boston, Philadelphia, Cincinnati and other major trading ports throughout the 1800s, New York became the dominant center for tea trade in America. This was due, in part, to the fact that by 1863, a twenty-five-cent tax was placed on each pound of tea as the government struggled to fund the Civil War. That duty had to be paid in gold, and gold had to be acquired on Wall Street. To be connected with tea during this era was considered a great distinction, for this line of business would generate a considerable fortune.

One businessman who saw this potential was George Gilman. He opened a store in New York City in 1863 called the Great American Tea Company that sold coffee, tea, sugar and spices. By 1866, his tea company was worth $1 million. The single business operated as two distinct companies with two different addresses, one for the Great American Tea Company and one for the Great Atlantic & Pacific Tea Company (A&P), located in the same corner building. Gilman was the marketing genius who launched the company to be, at one point, the largest tea dealer in America and who started the first grocery store chain. In 1880, A&P debuted Thea-Nectar, a brand name when brands were still rare. It was unusual in that it was sold exclusively at the A&P Grocery Store (Great Atlantic & Pacific Tea Company). Around

1872, he began offering coupons in his packaged tea that the customers could collect and redeem for china or glassware.

All of these teas, coffees and other beverages were being sold in taverns and restaurants, and these establishments were dominated by men. Unaccompanied women were not welcome in these places at all; the social custom of the late 1800s dictated that a woman had to be accompanied by a male escort if she visited any of these places. If she was not accompanied by a male escort, then she was not considered respectable and was not allowed to eat in the establishment. Eating in these establishments was uncomfortable for women and placed their respectability in jeopardy.

In the early 1900s, tea rooms became the answer for these respectable women. Women were starting to demand greater independence—in literature, in education, in the workplace and in society. They also began to seek more political power. The tea room, which served no alcohol and had a homelike atmosphere, gave women the chance to dine out—without that male escort or the worry of the results of diners being served alcohol. Women felt comfortable in tea rooms, which prided themselves on serving no alcohol and healthy, lighter and fresher fare than the meals served in taverns and restaurants. Women also had a difficult time finding lavatories outside their own homes at this time, and tea rooms accommodated this need, too. While most women think nothing of dining out without a man today, this was not always the case. Tea rooms played a major role in bringing about this change in society.

Many of these early tea rooms began in small rooms in a woman's house and catered to travelers. These tea rooms were owned and managed by women who found it easy to enter this particular world of business, having done this work for years without pay. Opening and maintaining a tea room played an integral part in allowing women to become part of the business world as entrepreneurs in what was essentially a man's world. Maine women became owners, managers and workers of tea rooms. These tea rooms gave women respectability and business and financial independence.

Goodwill-Hinckley Farm and Tea Room, Fairfield (1934)

In 1888, Mr. G.W. Hinckley started the Goodwill Farm in Fairfield to offer a home for orphans and needy children. By 1913, he had acquired five

Goodwill-Hinckley Tea Room. *Collections of L.C. Bates Museum/Good Will–Hinckley Homes, MHS 25876.*

hundred acres of land and had a total of thirteen structures to serve the two hundred children living there. A well-respected institute, it was visited by many people to view the efficiency of the Goodwill Farm to promote it as a great place for families to adopt the children staying there. It became such a popular destination that Hinckley's granddaughter Harriet Hinckley Price started the Goodwill Tea Room in 1934 to provide some refreshments for all the visitors, staff and local folks. An attractive individual house with a very pleasant view of the rolling hills and farmland on the Goodwill Farm property, this tea room did very well and served good, wholesome food to its many visitors. Today, it is standing as a private residence.

TEA ROOMS

Tea rooms of the early 1900s became all the rage across the country and especially in the vacation land of Maine. These tea rooms had a great influence on the community and the culture of the time. Their aim was to provide a respectable, elegant environment for women. Women bought, rented or borrowed barns, houses, gristmills, stores and more to serve as makeshift tea rooms. Cooking and other food preparation would take place in the home or over tiny stoves, which required bringing all their supplies from home. However, rural tea rooms had low overhead, lower labor costs and higher profits, which was very enticing to women entering the business world for the first time. Owning and managing a tea room ensured women that they could enjoy a pleasant, dignified and enjoyable profession with annual profits. Running a tea room involved menu planning, recipes, equipment buying, portion control, accounting, the hiring of employees and the selling of products. A skilled tea room manager commanded respect and admiration of all and had an enviable social position within the community.

Salmon Falls Tea Room, Hollis Center (1911–Present)

Situated right next to the Saco River is a building that is listed in the National Register of Historic Places. In 1911, this building was established as the Salmon Falls Village Library and Tea Room.

Salmon Falls Tea Room, Hollis Center. *Author photo.*

It had been purchased by noted author and educator Kate Douglas Wiggin for the sole purpose of establishing a library and tea room for the people of the town. She was a strong believer in literacy and felt everyone should have access to books. The first floor held the tea room and was managed by Mrs. Moses Davis and Mrs. William Moulton. It provided a very pleasant place to have a cup of tea while visiting with neighbors and borrowing books. Kate Douglas Wiggin was the author of the beloved children's books *The Birds' Christmas Carol*, published in 1887, and *Rebecca of Sunnybrook Farm*, published in 1903. These were so popular that they are still being published today. In 1934, the library was given to the town by Wiggin, stipulating that it remain a library and a place for community and children's events, which it is to this day.

Tea rooms became so popular that in addition to afternoon teas, they were also used as meeting places in the women's movements of temperance and suffrage, for entertainment venues for ladies' social clubs and for educating the public on the pleasures of the various teas and their medicinal qualities. When women learned to drive the automobile and safe public transportation became available in the form of trolleys, the tea rooms became even more popular. Prohibition banned alcohol, and this also made tea rooms very popular. New and better roads to the countryside and the seashore and the many tea rooms springing up gave modern women a way to join this twentieth-century tea movement. Traveling on weekends to the tea rooms of the country and seashore became so popular that road maps were even printed to help them find the best tea houses. These tea rooms were usually decorated with colonial furniture, hooked rugs and antiques. The enterprising tea room proprietor supplemented her income by offering these antiques for sale to her customers. The popular decorating fad of the colonial era represented a warmer, comfortable and more hospitable time to both men and women of this era.

Tea room managers and owners could attend management courses where they could learn the finer points of making a good cup of tea. They learned that tea has always been a symbol of culture and sophistication and that the first tea was green tea. Black tea was made by allowing the newly picked green tea leaves to oxidize by leaving them overnight. Originally, tea was loose leaf and was so expensive it was kept in locked boxes called tea caddies. Women were taught that tea can be only as good as the water it was made with, and once a tea was brewed, it was important to keep it hot. Tea cozies accomplished this. They first appeared in the eighteenth century but enjoyed a great comeback in the twentieth century as ladies began making their own cozies as parts of the arts and crafts movement. They were also instructed that leaving tea itself for too long in hot water resulted in a harsh and bitter brew. These management courses also frowned on the making of tea using the new invention of the tea bag. Loose tea made better tea. It was also taught that it was most ill-bred to refuse a cup of tea when it was offered to you. To indicate that you have had a sufficient amount of tea and did not want any more, you must place your spoon horizontally across the top of the cup.

JORDAN POND TEA HOUSE, SEAL HARBOR (1895–PRESENT)

This lovely tea house, famous for its popovers, is an institution in the tourist area of Bar Harbor and has the distinction of being the longest operating tea house in the state of Maine. Built in 1847, the original farmhouse was built by the

Jordan Pond Tea House. *Collections of Great Harbor Maritime Museum, MHS 22078.*

Jordan family of Seal Harbor, after whom the house and pond were named. In 1895, Thomas and Nellie McIntire purchased the old Jordan farm and turned it into a popular tea house. This location, by the end of the nineteenth century, had become a highly popular recreational area for summer vacationers. Its many customers have included presidents, foreign dignitaries, royalty, artists, locals and tourists. The McIntires developed the atmosphere and character of the original Jordan Pond House, which was noted for its birch bark dining and tea rooms with their massive fieldstone fireplaces.

The first popovers and tea were made by Nellie McIntire in 1895.

John D. Rockefeller purchased the property in 1928 and donated it to the National Park Service in 1940 after the McIntires retired from fifty years of continuous seasons of operation of the tea house. In 1946, Rockefeller began a company to oversee operating the Jordan Pond Tea House to ensure that the tradition of lunch, tea and popovers would continue, which it does to this very day.

Tea provided a focus for healthier living to all instead of the unhealthy alcohol that was being consumed in men's establishments. As a result of this, temperance societies against alcohol consumption sprang up all over the country and especially in Maine, and they held their meetings in local tea rooms. A sign in the tea room window would advertise "T" Room. The "T" was a code word for temperance. Groups of women felt safe entering a tea house, where they would not be subjected to diners who were consuming alcohol.

With the temperance meetings, tea rooms became hotbeds for women seeking social change and independence. They provided the ideal meeting place, especially for the women's suffrage movement. The first women's rights conference in America was held in Seneca Falls, New York, and it all began with an afternoon tea attended by five women determined to hold a convention about the injustices suffered by women. One of these women was Susan B. Anthony, who spoke in Maine about women's suffrage, encouraging women to support the cause while socially enjoying their tea.

Just over a half century later, tea was again linked to women's suffrage. A woman named Alva Vanderbilt Belmont, who occasionally spent summers in Maine, owned a mansion in Newport, Rhode Island, where she was considered the highest of society's hostess for Newport and New York City. At her Newport house, known as Marble House, she had an authentic Chinese tea house constructed in 1913. The building seated over one hundred guests and was used as a fundraising venue for women's suffrage. She also had porcelain dishes produced bearing the words "Votes for Women." Holding tea parties for hundreds of women and offering teacups and saucers for sale with these words written on them raised thousands of dollars for the suffrage

Quilt tea display. *Author photo.*

movement. Her contribution, through the use of tea, helped to achieve the passage of the Nineteenth Amendment to the U.S. Constitution giving women the right to vote. Seeing what Alva Vanderbilt Belmont was achieving inspired the women of Maine to start promoting suffrage by holding teas and also raising money for the cause. Some suffragettes even ran tea rooms themselves to raise money, usually located in department stores, where they offered for sale a specially packaged tea called Equality Tea. They offered homemade foods that reinforced the idea of home cooking and the idea that suffragettes were feminine women who deserved the vote. Men were warmly invited to patronize these suffragette tea rooms since they would be the ones deciding whether women would get the vote or not. When they came in for a good, cheap lunch, they would be handed a cup of tea and a suffragette brochure talking about the vote.

Dan Sing Fan Tea House and Gift Shop, Ogunquit (1934–2000)

The pagoda-like buildings of the Dan Sing Fan Tea House and Gift Shop were part of Ogunquit's Perkins Cove area for seventy-five years. Chauffer-driven limousines were continuously dropping off customers for lunch, tea or dinner at this fine establishment. With its Oriental-style décor, including Japanese lanterns, and the wonderful view of the ocean, this unique tea room's attractive highly lacquered red tables were always full of patrons. A gift shop included Maine handicrafts, Far East fashions and amber jewelry.

Dan Sing Fan Tea Room, Ogunquit. *Author collection.*

In addition to its fine food, it was noted for the best cinnamon toast in the area and famous for its checkerboard black-and-white fudge cake. The tea house was built by Richard Coolidge and his partner, Luigi Balestro, and they ran it for thirty-five years. It flourished until the 1960s. As one of Ogunquit's most popular dining establishments, it was always featured in every Maine resort guidebook, attracting a large clientele.

In 1964, Richard's adopted son, Osvaldo, changed the tea house menu into one featuring northern Italian cuisine and changed the name to Cove Garden, and he and his wife ran it for thirty-eight years. Its final ending was as a controlled burn as part of a training exercise by the Ogunquit Fire Department in the 2000s.

Most of these tea rooms offered good, inexpensive lunches like salmon with egg sauce, soups and stews; sandwiches such as pimento cheese, sliced chicken or cucumber; or waffles with maple syrup. Salad combinations were either fruit, chicken or celery with pineapple. Desserts were tea cakes, pies, toasted muffins, cinnamon toast, date bars or cookies. For afternoon tea, cinnamon toast was the most popular choice to pair with a cup of tea; all of the tea rooms offered this as a staple. Tea, toast and atmosphere were the essence of the tea room. Authentic tea houses were those that served "real toast" that was thick, soft and crusty. The club sandwich owed its popularity to being on real toast. Many patrons chose cinnamon toast and tea as the ideal afternoon tea menu. Some dishes promised a surprise like the tomato surprise, which was usually a whole tomato stuffed with chicken salad and served on a bed of lettuce. You might also find finger sandwiches. Maine tea houses always offered fresh produce grown in their own country gardens or seafood fresh from the waters of Maine. You were nearly always guaranteed a great home-cooked meal. The beverage list offered hot teas like Twinings Earl Grey or Orange Pekoe, ice-cold lemonade, grape juice or coffee. But the most popular drink was iced tea. And it had to be made a certain way, according to the McDonald Tea Room of Gallatin, Missouri, in 1938, as quoted in the book *A Social History of Tea*:

> *We make our tea using the cold-water method. Use 2 oz. of loose Orange Pekoe Tea to a gallon of cold water. Place loose tea in a cheesecloth bag and then place this bag in the water in a china, glass, or porcelain container. Let set for 24 hours in the refrigerator. It will color up in less time, but it takes*

> *this long to give it the clear brilliance of bourbon whiskey. It never clouds or darkens and has a fine flavor. Make Tuesday's supply of tea on Monday and thereafter each day tea is needed.*

It did not matter where the tea room was located; each had its own unique look and charm, and they were all successful. Modern tea rooms seem to focus on the Victorian era and reflect the interest of the twenty-first-century woman, while the twentieth-century tea rooms were decorated in the colonial period that symbolized a warmer, hospitable time to those tea room owners of the early 1900s.

For many years, tea rooms continued bringing pleasure to their customers until World War II. The advancement of a fast-paced life and the introduction of fast-food restaurants contributed to the decline of the tea rooms of yesterday.

SILVER BELL TEA ROOM, TURNER (1927–1940s)

The Silver Bell Tea Room was a very successful tea room that had the good fortune to be located on Route 4, a major thoroughfare, in the town of Turner. Locals and travelers passing through this area enjoyed the delicious home-cooked meals served there by owners Hortense and Freeland Beedy. This was a family-run business, which included their three sons, and everyone worked to make the business a success.

They made and sold their own butter, milk, desserts, pies and garden produce from their farm. A big customer favorite was their homemade ice cream. If you wanted the best chicken roll around, then the place to go was the Silver Bell Tea Room. Even Maine senator Edmund S. Muskie stopped there for a delicious home-cooked meal when traveling through the area.

An unusual feature of the tea room was its décor. The dining area showcased a few treasures of the family's taxidermy hobby. A squirrel, two partridge, a deer head with antlers and even a small bear cub graced the interior of the dining area, to the delight of customers. The business closed after many prosperous years due to the onset of World War II, the reduction of trade and the lack of adequate staff due to enlistment of the three sons to fight in the war.

Today, the Silver Bell Tea Room has been given a new life by the Beedys' great-great-granddaughter Heather Nadeau. She and her husband have

Silver Bell Tea Room, Turner. *Author photo.*

restored the tea room to a beautiful, charming building that will soon become a wine-tasting venue, not far from the original location of the notable Silver Bell Tea Room.

Today, tea is making a strong comeback as a refreshing drink in Maine and nationwide. Brands such as Celestial Seasonings, Stash, Twinings, Tazo Tea, the Republic of Tea and green teas are all popular in many of today's tea rooms, coffee houses and restaurants. Teas and tea rooms are so popular now that they are creating phenomenal growth in specialty teas, green teas, tea ware designs, tea companies, tea rooms, tea shops, tea bars, classes, books, magazines and websites.

Tea and tea rooms forever changed the way America eats out and laid the groundwork for the modern small restaurant and coffee bar.

These tea rooms also helped create a profound social change in our society by helping to promote women's independence. Tea, today, has achieved an image as a true gourmet beverage that is part of a healthy lifestyle, and modern tea rooms promote that fact.

One-half of today's American population drink teas, with the largest concentration of tea drinkers in the Northeast and South. Interestingly, 85 percent of the tea consumed is iced, and over 65 percent is prepared using teabags.

In today's fast-paced world, tea has become a ritual for slowing down and enjoying a calm respite from the hustle and bustle of our world. It also allows us to capture some of the charm of the historic tea rooms of earlier times by taking the time to enjoy that soothing, delicious cup of tea. Whether at a tea bar, tea room or in our own home, the sampling of today's many varieties of tea brings us as much pleasure as it did our ancestors. The purpose and environment in these establishments continue to promote the many benefits of sharing a cup of tea in an atmosphere that reflects two of our country's great established accomplishments: women's independence and sociability for all.

THE PLEASURE OF AFTERNOON TEA

Imagine, if you will, a pretty little tea room surrounded by fragrant, sweet-smelling pine or glowing birch trees. You are seated by the window with a spectacular view of the ocean, the sun is shining and you are enjoying a tall, cooling glass of delicious iced tea with a friend.

The interesting history of tea, the social happenings of afternoon teas and the development of the extremely popular tea rooms all led to America's great romance with the social custom of relaxing and sharing a cup of tea with a friend. This was true even in the early years of the state of Maine. Mainers have been drinking tea as a beverage since the late 1600s and have been involved with tea in some form since then, as consumers, in the shipping industry or as craftsmen making tea caddies, tea tables and teapots.

By the 1600s, tea was available in America. Because of the high price of importing tea at this time, it was only enjoyed by the upper class. The equipment used to make tea at this time would have included a tea table, a teapot, a sugar bowl, a creamer, cups and saucers and a kettle full of hot water. In addition to these items, due to the very high cost of tea, a tea box or caddy that locked was necessary. In fact, it was the most important item in the household. Tea was traditionally brewed and poured by the hostess, not her servant, due to the high cost, and only she would select and remove the tea from the caddy.

During the late 1700s and early 1800s, the numerous tea caddies found in various households was a strong indication that tea was becoming a favorite drink for all. The word *caddy* did not originally refer to a container. It was a measure of weight called a *kati*, which was a Chinese weight of measurement that was the equivalent of one and a half pounds, which is how much a tea caddy would hold. Most early tea caddies were made of wood, silver or tin, and all had a lock and key to keep the tea safe from pilfering. With green tea and *Bohea* (black) tea being the most popular kinds of tea, many of these caddies had two separate compartments to keep the teas separated. Sometimes these compartments held canisters to hold the tea. By the 1800s, a third space was being added within the box to hold a sugar bowl or container.

Many of these tea caddies were imported, with some being made by local craftsmen. These could be inlaid with rich woods and have decorative paintings or engravings on them that added to their beauty. Some of them contained covers for the separate containers inside to prevent the tea from drying out. A velvet-covered center section would be provided to hold the sugar bowl. Trade with the Orient during this time provided lacquered tea caddies fitted with Chinese decorated removable containers. There were also caddies from China made from a metal called *paktong*, which was an alloy composed of copper, nickel and zinc that gave off a soft sheen that did not need polishing. By the 1840s, this metal was being replaced by silver. With so many caddies available, tea caddies were not only necessary, but they also added to the décor of the home, especially when they began to be made of porcelain.

During the years of the American Revolutionary War, tea was boycotted, and other replacements were sought. Maine homemakers turned to their gardens and orchards for suitable substitutes and called them Liberty Teas. The leaves of plants like spearmint, peppermint, orange bergamot, lemon balm, raspberry, blueberry and apples were some of the tastier ones for teas. Chamomile, sage and rosehips also proved popular. An article in the *Boston Gazette* of 1768 offered this suggestion: "Tea made from a plant or shrub (*ceanothus americanus*) grown in Pearstown [present-day Standish] about 20 miles from Portland, Maine, was served to a circle of ladies and gentlemen in Newbury Port, who pronounced it nearly, if not quite, it's equal in flavor to genuine Bohea tea. If we have the plant, nothing is wanted but the process of curing it into 'tea' of our own manufacture."

PERCY HILL GARDENS AND TEA ROOM, AUGUSTA (1915)

A beautiful setting for an outdoor garden tea room was established in 1915 on the grounds of the Percy Vickery Hill estate located on State Street in Augusta. Percy Hill, the son of Governor John Fremont Hill, was an

Percy Hill Gardens and Tea Room. *Collections of Maine Historical Society, MHS 14562.*

Augusta publisher and businessman noted for helping found the Augusta Country Club with fellow investors Guy Gannett and Walter S. Wyman.

This palatial mansion was designed by Charles N. Cogswell of Boston in the Colonial style, containing twenty-three rooms and six bathrooms. The cost to build this lovely home was $100,000, which included a cavernous ballroom on the third floor and all the furnishings of the house. The grounds on the estate covered four acres and were designed by Carl Rust Parker of Portland. Three twenty-foot-wide terraces led from the house to the garden. The garden itself was forty feet by eighty feet with a center pool filled with lilies and fish. The tea room, built of brick, was located at the southeast end of the garden. This beautiful tea room had an open air to it and overlooked the extensive garden, bringing pleasure to all who used it. It was mainly used for family functions and social events at the mansion.

A large variety of the teas made from native plants were a bit bitter, just as some of the imported teas were. To make the drink more palatable, people started adding a sweetener to the brewed tea. Refined white sugar was used by the wealthy, and dark brown unrefined sugar, molasses or honey was used by the poor. The sugar was used to reduce the bitterness of the tea, not just to sweeten it. Most people also put milk or cream in their tea by this time if they could afford it.

A story about the early method tried in preparing the tea leaves gives us some amusement today. In 1850, a pound of tea was received as a gift to the household without directions on how to prepare it. It was decided to boil the whole of it at once in a pot filled with water, which soon was done. They then sat down to eat the leaves, minus the liquid, with butter and salt. It was declared that this dish was decidedly inedible, and they were left wondering how anyone could ever like such a dish and threw it out without tasting the liquid!

By the early 1800s, tea was no longer an elegant upper-class beverage served only in drawing rooms by society ladies. It had become a drink that was enjoyed by everyone, regardless of class. Breakfast and the big noontime dinner, according to Maine custom, were usually family affairs, but late afternoon teas and suppers were often joined by friends and relatives. Teas varied from small meals of just tea with bread, butter and preserves to more elaborate meals with meat, sandwiches and even hot food. At late afternoon teas, ladies would be offered bread, butter, preserves and cake. If gentlemen were attending, then tea was offered with bread, cakes and meats.

Tea was now also becoming the symbol and focus point for the newly formed temperance movement. For years, alcohol, beer, ale and cider had been a large part of the daily diet, especially at mealtimes, because of unsafe drinking water. Excessive imbibing was accepted as normal behavior at this time. The evils and dangers associated with alcohol were just beginning to be realized. Drunken and bawdy behavior among the majority of the population, though common, was now becoming offensive to many and threatening to home life. People were now being encouraged to drink tea instead, as it was a refreshing drink that contained many medicinal qualities with no side effects such as you would get with alcohol. Portland, Maine, was the home of one of the nation's leaders in the temperance movement. Neil Dow was known as the Father of Temperance, and later, as a celebrated Union Civil War general, he used his influence to promote temperance. While serving in the Civil War, he was captured in 1863 and spent eight months in the infamous Libby Prison in Richmond, Virginia. In 1864, he was exchanged for Confederate general Fitzhugh Lee, son of Robert E. Lee. Shortly after his release, Dow resigned from the Union army and returned to Maine. During his time as mayor of Portland, he, in 1850, enacted the first temperance ordinances to pass in any American city. His wealth allowed him to build an elegant home at 714 Congress Street, where he developed an extensive library of books on temperance.

He shared this home with his daughter Cornelia Dow, who managed the household after her mother's death. She served on the executive committees of both the Maine Woman's Christian Temperance Union (WCTU) and the national organization. She was a quiltmaker and is noted for making a quilt with other ladies that contains patriotic, antislavery and temperance inscriptions on it. It is now in the permanent collection of the Maine State Museum in Augusta. As a strong member of the Maine WCTU, she participated in many temperance teas that included prominent speakers of the day encouraging temperance. Some of the temperance teas would most likely have been held in the Dows' mansion, which eventually was donated to the Maine WCTU by Neal's son and is today open to the public for tours.

Temperance teas were held throughout Maine communities. In 1917, the Woman's Christian Temperance Union presented a statue to the City of Portland in remembrance of Lillian Stevens, who was one of the founders of the Maine chapter of the WCTU. The *Little Water Girl* statue is now located at the Portland Public Library on Congress Street, a fitting tribute to Maine's temperance teas and Maine's involvement in the movement. Women were now giving speeches around the country to encourage teetotalism and total abstinence and to discourage drinking.

Members of the early temperance societies took a pledge of total abstinence and urged people to drink tea instead. The word *teetotal* was coined as a link between tea and alcohol. Alcohol-free fundraising meetings grew in popularity and attracted large numbers of attendees from one hundred to five hundred people wherever they were held and became a focus for healthier living. Women all over the country were joining and, surprisingly, even some men.

By the 1840s, temperance restaurants, hotels and tea rooms were coming into existence, offering inexpensive food with nonalcoholic drinks in safe, pleasant surroundings. Opening up all over the country, they had the added attraction of being the ideal place for ladies to hold their temperance meetings.

By the late 1800s, women began seeking more independence in their lives and were holding meetings to recruit members for the suffrage movement, just as they had for the temperance movement. There was public suffrage activity in Maine as early as 1854, when Susan B. Anthony spoke in Bangor. Women's rights meetings were being held throughout Maine, and by 1873, a statewide organization was formed at a convention in Augusta that included Julia Ward Howe, originator of the "Battle Hymn of the Republic," among its prominent speakers. As a result of this convention, the National Grange endorsed suffrage, favoring votes for women.

STANWOOD PARK, FARMINGTON

If you were looking for a cup of tea while exploring the Farmington area, you would most likely have headed for Stanwood Amusement Park. In addition to a tea room that also offered regular meals, the park had camping for tourists, a zoo and a dance hall.

This tea room may have been used for meetings, too, as were other tea rooms in Maine. Among the most important meetings to be held in these tea rooms were for promotion of women's suffrage. Tea rooms and grange halls provided the ideal meeting venues for the suffragettes. A resident of Farmington, Isabel Whittier Greenwood, frequently gave speeches at these venues encouraging women to join the suffragette movement and also to support the local grange organizations. Isabel was the wife of Chester Greenwood, the inventor of earmuffs. Chester also held a patent for the whistling tea kettle!

Isabel organized the Franklin County Equal Suffrage Association in February 1906. At these tea room meetings, she gave women of Franklin County the news on suffrage activity in the rest of the state and country, such as marches being held in Portland by suffragettes wearing long white dresses and white hats marching up State Street and down Congress Street all the way to city hall encouraging "Votes for Women." She worked tirelessly to recruit members for the state's suffrage association, as were other members working throughout the state. The tea rooms, again, became the ideal meeting place and an integral part of the women's liberation movement. These new tea rooms were very important for respectable women, as they offered safe, clean gathering places now that women were beginning to appear unescorted in more public places, such as shopping, using public transportation or attending social events. The suffrage movement not only allowed women to visualize the right to vote, but it also helped them visualize that they could run their own businesses—such as owning their own tea rooms!

Green Mountain Tea House at Acadia National Park, Bar Harbor (1880)

This tea house was built on the summit of Green Mountain in the town of Bar Harbor in 1880. It was one of the first tea houses to be built in Maine and the only one to be built on a mountain. Green Mountain is now known as Cadillac Mountain and is part of Acadia National Park. The tea room was eventually expanded and became known as the Green Mountain Hotel, which included the tea room. Guests could take the Green Mountain Cog Railway from the base of Eagle Lake up to the summit of the mountain to enjoy afternoon tea with a spectacular view of the ocean and surrounding area. It was a unique experience and very popular with the locals and tourists.

Farwell and Wight's Tea Room, Bethel (1923–1945)

This tea room was originally built as a store located on Church Street. Addie Roxy Bryant Farwell and her husband, William, purchased the store in 1923 and converted it into a tea room and small store. After both William and their daughter's husband, Walter Wight, died within nine days of each other in March 1924, their daughter, Lena Farwell Wight, joined her mother in the enterprise. They advertised that they were always open and could supply any

Farwell and White's Tea Room, Bethel. *Courtesy of Amy Wight Chapman.*

need. As a tea room, they catered to a first-class, extensive trade enjoyed by both locals and tourists. In a very short time, Farwell and Wight's Tea Room was very popular and became known for its delicious pies. This successful business pleased its many customers for years until 1945, when it was sold to Albert F. Cotton, who continued the business as a store and restaurant.

Many of Maine's early tea rooms run by women began in a room or two in the owner's own home. These tea rooms were open on the weekends to offer refreshments to travelers and tourists. The early 1900s saw the hugely popular sport of bicycling become a social craze that added greatly to the growing success of tea rooms. The bicycle craze attracted both men and women, so much so that bicycle clubs were formed, and thousands of bicyclists were now riding throughout the cities and countryside nearly every day. This, of course, created a need for refreshments, which presented the perfect opportunity to stop at the nearest tea room.

Old Grist Mill Tea Room, Kennebunkport (1940s–1994)

This tea room building on Mill Lane started its life as an actual working gristmill before it was converted into a tea room and restaurant. The Perkins Tide Mill was located on the north side of Kennebunkport Village, on the northeast shore of Mill Stream, a tidal arm of the Kennebunk River. The mill was built in 1749 by Captain Thomas Perkins. The original grindstone was imported from England, and the dam was originally granite with pine posts. A new grindstone was imported from France in 1866. The mill used the tides from the Kennebec River for power to grind corn into meal until closing down in 1937.

In 1939, the daughter of the last miller opened a tea room and then a restaurant in the building. It was opened and run by two generations of the Lombard family. When you entered the tea room, you could see a wide variety of equipment related to the history of its gristmill operations, including a waterwheel, grindstones and gears and shafts. The main dining room was bright and cheerful and overlooked Mill Stream, which provided wonderful

Old Grist Mill, Kennebunkport. *Author collection.*

views during the summer and fall. It was a seasonal tea room that was closed in the winter and spring, as there was not insulation or heat in the building. Popular with the public because of its uniqueness and its food, it remained open until 1994, when it burned down "under suspicious circumstances." In 2006, the property was acquired by the Kennebec Conservation Trust, which is presently working on plans to reconstruct the mill using timbers from period structures and parts from antique mills.

BLUE LANTERN TEA ROOM, SURRY (1946–1972)

The Blue Lantern Tea Room opened in 1946 just after World War II in Surry in conjunction with the Surry Playhouse. The playhouse offered some elegance and culture in a charming, rustic setting. The Surry Playhouse was a summer stock theater that first opened in 1929 but closed in 1939 as World War II was approaching. Shows were revivals of older classics or, often, recent Broadway hits. This little theater on the coast of Maine seated three hundred, and for those eleven years before World War II and in its sixteen years after reopening in 1946, it drew clientele from those summering on Mount Desert Island, Blue Hill, Castine and some of the local folks. All summer long, chauffeurs lined up in the circular driveway to deposit their well-dressed patrons for the theater and dinner.

Blue Lantern Tea Room. *Collections of Surry Historical Society, MHS 70723.*

A large part of the Surry Playhouse was the rustic outdoor tea room that began when the playhouse reopened in 1946, serving lunch, afternoon tea and dinner. The structure was an open-weave log roof over a solid floor with open sides, allowing one to experience dining out of doors to its fullest. Rough tables and small stools, both made from logs, made up the dining area, and each table featured a vase full of flowers of the day. In addition to dining, the Blue Lantern also offered pottery, textiles and antiques for sale, all while giving actors like Joseph Cotton and Henry Fonda their start in their early acting careers.

The Blue Lantern Tea Room closed in 1953, but the theater reopened as the New Surry Playhouse and Dinner Theatre in 1972. The new theater provides great summer entertainment and food to the present day.

THE WHISTLING OYSTER TEA ROOM, OGUNQUIT (1920S–1976)

The Whistling Oyster Tea Room, a very popular tea room located in the Perkins Cove area of Ogunquit, opened its doors in the 1920s. In addition to the tea room, a Christmas gift shop section of the building offered attractive gifts to purchase for the holidays.

The tea room was operated by Helen Ryan, and the Christmas gift shop was operated by Joy Hawley. The tea room advertised lunch from 12:00

to 2:00 p.m., tea from 3:30 to 5:00 p.m. and dinner from 6:00 to 8:30 p.m. Among the many items on the menu, it was noted for its cinnamon toast, rum cakes and the Whistling Oyster mint cup, and for fifty cents, you could request Captain Blight's Delight, served hot or cold, from the dinner menu. The tea room was so popular that reservations were required. In the Christmas gift shop, the specialty was long, personalized Christmas stockings, which were custom made by the owners. The tea room burned down in 1976. A new building was built on the site and is operating today as Barnacle Billy's Restaurant.

In Maine's rural areas and along the coast, owners of tea rooms took advantage of the fact that people were now making more and more excursions out of town by foot, bicycle or trolley. At these tea rooms, you might find pretty gardens, scenic views and delicious food, with especially refreshing cold drinks like iced tea. This was during the era before food safety and health laws were in effect, and women could make an income without leaving home. The Maine women who operated these tea rooms were very knowledgeable in preparing food and drinks for customers, as they had for years been preparing large meals for farm workers, church suppers and other social events—all without pay!

During this time, a colonial revival was taking place throughout the country. Colonial Williamsburg in Virginia was being created, causing great nationwide interest. People were also embracing the remembered comfort and love of their ancestors' way of life, which included colonial décor. Because of this, the Colonial Revival look became the dominant theme of the time, and tea rooms now used this theme as their main décor, especially in Maine, as a lot of these items were family pieces that enhanced the tea room's atmosphere. Wood, pewter, braided rugs and calico shared space with weather vanes, spinning wheels, copper kettles and antiques. Some tea rooms even used "Ye Olde" in their names to enhance the public's desire for all things colonial, and this drew many a happy audience.

A fair number of Maine's tea rooms were accessible to a lot of people for the price of a ticket on the trolley lines that traveled throughout ninety different communities in Maine. Riding a trolley to visit a tea room in the countryside or at the seashore was an enjoyable day-trip outing for many.

WILDWOOD INN AND TEA ROOM, CUMBERLAND (1909–1929)

The Wildwood Inn and Tea Room was on the trolley line and was located on fifty acres of land covered with fragrant, sweet-smelling pines extending from the Foreside Road (Route 88) in Cumberland down to the smooth, sandy beach at the water's edge. Its many attractions included a spectacular viewing with a six-hundred-foot dock for fishing and boating, swimming at the pool at the inn, two tennis courts, three bathhouses, a beach with a raft, a pier, diving chutes and a gazebo. Natural spring water was available along with the celebrated shore dinners.

This was a trolley stop as well as a steamboat stop. The roof of the inn had "Wildwood" painted on it so the steamboat ferry could see it in inclement weather. Customers for the dinner hour would enter the inn on the left side of the building, pay for their dinner, pass through the Japanese Room noted for its Oriental design and then proceed to the porch to enjoy their meals. The porch accommodated eight large round oak tables seating ten at each table with attractive bentwood chairs. Wildwood was celebrated for its notable shore and clam dinners, with the clams being dug from Wildwood's own beach.

The Japanese Room was, in all probability, the room designated for "afternoon teas" that were served. At that time, everything Japanese was considered fashionable décor to have for a tea room. Japanese tableware,

Wildwood Inn and Tea Room, Cumberland. *Courtesy of Cumberland Historical Society.*

such as teacups and teapots, would have been used, and a variety of teas along with sandwiches and desserts would have been offered for the diners' pleasure. A creative atmosphere such as this would have almost guaranteed that your tea room would be successful.

Wildwood was designed by Herman P. Rausch and Concord Realty, a land development corporation from New York, who purchased the land from Sumner Sturdivent, son of Ephriam Sturdivent, an early Cumberland sea captain.

The Wildwood Inn and Tea Room served the public for many years until the automobile made the trolleys obsolete and diminished the patronage of the tea room. It closed in 1929.

PRIDE'S FOREST TEA ROOM, WEST CUMBERLAND (1920S–1940S)

Twelve miles from Portland, a tea room was built at the intersection of Route 100 and Blackstrap Road in West Cumberland. Research has shown that it was most likely owned and operated by the Pride family who lived nearby on Bruce Hill Road. The tea room was situated on a beautiful setting of dense growth pine and birch trees and was always flying an American flag. This

Pride's Forest Tea Room interior, West Cumberland. *Courtesy of Cumberland Historical Society.*

tea room was on a major road, and patrons arrived by automobile or by the interurban trolley.

One of its major attractions was that it was located within walking distance of Forest Lake for an enjoyable day's outing ending with a stop for refreshments at the tea room. If you were arriving by automobile, then the gas station on the grounds of the tea room would ensure you could continue your travels after enjoying a meal. The tea room was noted for its delicious hot waffles and chicken pie.

A large screened-in porch on two sides of the building offered seating at round tables with bentwood chairs, all under a grass hut–like ceiling. If it was a chilly day outside, then the attractive stone fireplace at one end of the dining room would be lit to make your dining a bit more comfortable. The Pride's Forest Tea Room was a fine contribution to its community and was enjoyed by its many patrons.

Casco Bay Tea Room, Yarmouth (1930s–1940s)

This tea room was built in the mid-1930s in Yarmouth by Harry Dean. It was built at the former location of the Yarmouth Trolley waiting room located at the base of Marina Road at the intersection with Route 88. Locally, it was also known as Dean's Tea Room. It served local patrons as well as tourists. This tea room was one of the few that survived after the discontinuation of trolley services, even though it was located on a trolley line. Duncan Hines, a restaurant guidebook writer of the 1930s and 1940s, recommended tea rooms as the best places to eat, as they served fine home cooking. In 1937, Hines reported that a local man said of the Casco Bay Tea Room, "Don't be afraid of the name tea room, its food is fine home cooking." Duncan Hines always took the presence of men in a tea room as proof of its good quality. The tea room closed sometime in the 1940s. The building has since housed a shoe store, an antique store, a gift shop and offices. Today, the building is enjoying a renewed life as the very successful and in vogue business of Sara Sullivan, certified nutritionist, which offers client consultations and nutritional cooking classes. It is a very fitting business for this building that began its life as a popular tea room offering the best quality of food and nutrition to its customers, as Sara Sullivan does today!

Casco Bay Tea Room, Yarmouth. *Author photo.*

Another popular trolley excursion was the delightful pastime at the turn of the century of a day spent at the nearest trolley resort park. Visiting one of Maine's trolley parks for the day became hugely popular, and each park featured a tea room that was one of the busiest entertainments at the park.

Riverton Trolley Park, Portland (1896–1921)

This forty-acre park offered both day and nighttime amusements. There were shelters for picnics, a carousel, croquet lawns, a petting zoo, trout ponds for fishing, a bandstand, a restaurant, a tea room and a rustic outdoor amphitheater featuring vaudeville acts and seating for 2,500 people. A big enjoyment was the dance hall with live orchestras playing.

Frank Blaisdell, designer of Boston Public Gardens, was the designer for Riverton Trolley Park, which included numerous flower gardens, broad lawns, arches, arbors and rustic bridges. It was opened in 1896 by the Portland Railroad Company to attract customers to its trolley. People got on the trolley at Monument Square in Portland to be taken out to the many attractions at Riverton Trolley Park, including its popular casino. The casino featured card rooms, a restaurant, a tea room and smoking rooms. There was also a wharf at the park where one could board a steamboat for a leisurely ride on the Presumpscot River. The trolley park lasted for twenty-five years until 1921 before closing its doors because of decreased business due to the automobile and World War I. The casino was torn down in 1933.

Casco Castle, Freeport (1902–1914)

This trolley park offered a day full of elegance and excitement. In fact, you could even enjoy a longer stay, as this park offered accommodations for overnight guests in its many rooms and was a very popular destination for day trippers and vacationers. In addition to a fine restaurant, the castle also had a lovely tea room. For entertainment, you were offered dancing, musical performances, moonlit sails, tours of formal gardens, baseball, swimming, tennis, a small zoo, rooftop gardens and concerts.

It was built to look like a small castle, complete with a moat and a one-hundred-foot-tall tower. You would disembark from the trolley and then walk

Casco Castle. *Collections of Maine Historical Society, MHS 17413.*

across the three-hundred-foot expansion bridge that spanned the Spar Creek deep ravine to reach the castle. Broad piazzas extended entirely around the building on the second and third floors. The castle could house one hundred guests and was served by the Harpswell Steamboat Company as well as the trolleys that delivered guests daily.

A popular summertime excursion was to take the steamer from Portland to South Freeport in the morning, spend some time at the castle in the afternoon and then return to Portland by trolley in the evening.

The Casco Castle was built by the "Electric Railway King," Amos Fitz Gerald, in 1902, the same man who built Merrymeeting Park in Brunswick. The castle was destroyed by fire in September 1914, but the tower still stands today.

LAKE GROVE TROLLEY PARK, AUBURN (1890–1928)

This beautiful trolley park was situated on Lake Auburn and was called Lake Grove. It was built in 1890 and ran until 1928, when the automobile became more popular. If you wanted a fun-filled day's outing, then you would spend it at Lake Grove Trolley Park in Auburn. This park offered a full day's amusement for everyone. It had a magic lantern theater, horseshoe courts, croquet lawns, bowling alleys, roller skating and a curiosity museum. You could have a tintype photo taken of yourself and your friends, have a picnic and then rent a canoe or rowboat for a pleasurable afternoon. If you preferred, steamboat cruises around Lake Auburn were also available. The restaurant there offered wonderful shore dinners, and afternoon teas could be had at the tea room, topped off by band concerts, both day and night. A wonderful day to be had by all who attended.

ANOTHER GREAT BOOST TO the popularity of the tea room's allure came with the public's fascination with the invention of the automobile. Modern women were learning how to drive the automobile, alcohol was banned due to Prohibition laws and, finally, more and better roads were being built. These three things created the perfect scenario for the twentieth-century tea movement and enhanced tea rooms to a very desirable destination in the social world of the early 1900s. It became a common occurrence for a group of ladies, a family or a group of friends to motor to the countryside or the seashore in their automobile in search of a day's adventure, which always included a stop at a tea room for a lunch of chicken salad, iced tea and a variety of desserts—all homemade!

WESTCUSTAGO INN AND TEA ROOM, YARMOUTH (1920–2006)

The original building of the Westcustago Inn and Tea Room was built around 1920 by Ernest Percy Johnson and began as a tea room with one kitchen and one dining room. A large sun porch was added in 1921, with later expansions to the dining areas over the years increasing the dining capacity significantly from the original structure.

The Johnson family ran the business while living on the site, and there were also quarters for some of the staff on the property. The Westcustago was known far and wide for its fine food, especially lobster dinners.

Wescustago Inn and Tea Room, Yarmouth. *Author photo.*

Customers came from all over to enjoy the many specialties offered. It was so well known that it even attracted a number of celebrities who were passing through the area, such as Jean Harlow, Joe Louis, Clark Cable, Gary Merrill, Bette Davis and Franklin and Eleanor Roosevelt. Eleanor was known for enjoying her cup of tea and in later years in her political life was known to quote that "a woman is like a tea bag—you never know how strong she is until you put her in hot water!"

The Westcustago Inn and Tea Room was sold in 1942. The business changed hands numerous times, always operating as a restaurant, until 2006, when it was sold once again. It is currently the home of Cunningham Security.

The Vanity Fair Tea Room, Surry (1930s)

The Vanity Fair Tea Room and Guest House was built in 1850 as the home for Edwin and Edna Goodwin in the town of Surry. This lovely small town was home to the Surry Playhouse, which opened its barn doors to the public in 1929. It was a summer theater that enjoyed a wonderful audience for its Broadway productions. After a number of years, this house and property was sold to Gertrude Minnigerode of Baltimore, Maryland, who ran it as a tea room and guest house with herself serving as the hostess. The tea room had a loyal following, as the specialty was southern cuisine, which was not often found in Maine at that time. It also contained a well-stocked gift shop that pleased both locals and tourists.

Traveling by automobile occurred so frequently now that road maps were even printed that informed you of the locations of the very best tea rooms and antique shops to visit as you explored the various areas during your day trips. A good number of tea rooms in Maine also offered their customers homemade jams and jellies, jars of pickles, breads and whole pies for sale, along with handmade quilts, a variety of needlework and antiques for all the day trippers to purchase.

LANIER CRAFT AND TEA SHED, ELIOT (1903–1940)

Built on the lands of the Leighton estate on the River Road in Eliot, the Lanier Craft and Tea Shed was part of what was known as the Lanier Camp. Consisting of fifty acres of waterside, meadow and woodlands, it was one of the first coeducational camps for children in the country. The widow of noted poet Sidney Lanier, their children and their grandchildren all helped operate the camp. The camp included homes and other buildings on both sides of the road. Cecil Sharp, who founded the English Folk Dance Society and brought Morris dancing to the United States in 1914, first demonstrated and taught it here at the Lanier Camp in 1915. Morris dancing is a form of English folk dance accompanied by music. It is based on rhythmic stepping with the group of dancers wearing bell pads on their shins. Sticks, swords or handkerchiefs may also be used by the dancers. The earliest forms of Morris dancing date to 1448.

The tea room was located in the middle of the camp in an existing barn. Painted red with wonderful large windows on two sides of the Tea Shed, it featured French glass doors that led to a large glass-enclosed porch for

Lanier Craft and Tea Shed, Eliot. *Author photo.*

dining and then outside to lovely gardens where concerts were frequently held. Inside were smart-looking tables and chairs arranged to host quite a number of guests. The usual tea room menu consisting of sandwiches, desserts and tea was offered along with a variety of crafts produced at the camp, including jams and jellies, cards, artwork and imports. The camp and tea room closed in 1940.

THE CHEERYNEUK TEA ROOM, ELIOT (1930–1940)

A very popular tea room was established in the town of Eliot in 1930, to the delight of the local residents and tourists who were exploring southern Maine. It was located on River Road in Eliot and housed in a barn on the old Stacy property. A scenic road would lead you up to the very rustic-looking barn that offered something for everyone in the way of refreshments. Hot tea was served, with iced tea available in the warmer months. Cold milk, juice, sandwiches, cakes and the ever-present cinnamon toast were always a standard on the menu.

The tea room was owned by two maiden ladies, Edna Thomas and Melanie Murdock. Edna was the great-granddaughter of Seth Thomas,

Cheeryneuk Tea Shed, Eliot. *Author collection.*

the originator of the prestigious Seth Thomas Clock Company. The town of Thomaston, Maine, was named for her family. Melanie was from New York and was a very accomplished weaver. Her tapestries added to the décor of the inside of the charming tea room. After ten years of successful business, the tea room was sold and was dearly missed by all its loyal customers.

Once the automobile was established in people's lives, the world became a lot more mobile. People were traveling for business reasons, to attend meetings, for vacations or for shopping excursions and enjoying tea at tea rooms along the way.

Arcadia Tea Room at Lakewood Theatre, Lakewood (1901–Present)

In the town of Lakewood, near Madison and Skowhegan, lies a well-known Maine theater and restaurant. Driving down the road lined with birch and pine trees to the end, you arrive at the shores of Lake Wesserunsett and the Lakewood Theatre complex. Established in 1901, it is said to be the oldest and finest summer stock theater company in America with a Broadway cast.

The theater and complex was the vision of Bangor native Herbert L. Swett. In its most popular years between 1925 and 1941, the theater was a major summer tryout for productions hoping for success on Broadway. One of the longest-running plays on Broadway, *Life with Father*, premiered at Lakewood in 1939. Comedies, dramas, musicals and children's shows are presented there. In 1921, a tea room was built across from the theater to accommodate theatergoers.

The tea room was managed by Francer Swett, wife of Lakewood's owner, and it offered luncheons, afternoon teas and dinners. In 1924, a large room with a fireplace was added, and it was advertised as a "winter picnic" spot for ice skating parties. In 1926, an even larger facility was needed, and the original tea room was razed and replaced by a new, larger restaurant built on the same site, incorporating the tea room.

Arcadia Tea Room at Lakewood Theatre, Lakewood. *Author photo.*

Numerous Broadway celebrities have starred at the Lakewood, including Mama Cass Elliot, Carol Burnett and John Travolta. Lakewood Theatre was designated the State Theater of Maine by the Maine legislature in 1968, and it was added to the National Register of Historic Places on June 18, 1975.

LIBBY'S COLONIAL TEA ROOM, WELLS (1923–1942)

In the spring of 1923, a new bungalow-style dining room was built for and operated as a tea room for local tourists traveling along U.S. Route 1 in Wells. It was built and operated by a resourceful woman named Elsie Klingman Libby, who was forty-one years old when she opened the tea room. This tea room replaced a previous restaurant owned by Libby at the same location that had burned down in 1922. This well-known and popular tea room was known far and wide as a fine dining establishment. It was also known for its function space that was used by many local organizations for their dinner meetings. Since its location was on U.S. Route 1 in Wells, the

Libby's Colonial Tea Room, Wells. *Author photo.*

principal corridor, the tea room also did a brisk tourist business. Among the names in the guest book is that of then New York governor Franklin Delano Roosevelt, who signed it on October 31, 1932, during his campaign that resulted in his first election as president.

The tea room remained in operation until the effect of the decreased tourist trade and World War II forced its closure. Today, it has a new life as the Johnson Hall Museum located at the junction of U.S. Route 1 and Harraseeket Road in Wells.

Owners were encouraged to strive for refinement and elegance when choosing a name for their tea room. Names like the Crystal Lilac Tea Room or the Beach Rose Tea Room would help to ensure its success, while names like the Green Moth Tea Room or the Chase-'em-in Tea Room probably would not.

Bonnie Brig Tea Room, Kennebunkport (1900–60s)

The advertising brochure for this lovely tea room stated, "The gift shops and tea rooms which one finds so plentiful at the different resorts are not usually conducted in so 'up-to-date' style as the popular 'Bonnie Brig,' hence its great popularity with hotel guests and cottagers of Kennebunkport and neighboring beaches."

It must have been very popular, as a letter dated June 14, 1957, from the Bonnie Brig Tea Room to Winslow Randall of Redlands, California, finally arrived at his post office box fifty-seven years later! Randall, who died in the 1980s, was a phenomenal bridge player who had written to the Bonnie Brig Tea Room inquiring about room rates. The reply from the Bonnie Brig states that rooms could be reserved for eight dollars per night with a shared bath or ten dollars per night with a private bath—both with meals included. The letter was delivered to Steve Spiller, who had Randall's previous post office box for thirty-three years and said that its delivery was delayed due to an incorrect zip code.

The Bonnie Brig Tea Room's policy was satisfaction guaranteed. In addition to an experienced management staff, they also did catering to the very best of trade. The tea room offered rooms for rent; packed to go

Bonnie Brig Tea Room, Kennebunkport. *Author collection.*

lunches for boat excursions or trips; made to-order cakes for birthdays, celebrations or afternoon teas; and offered a well-stocked gift shop where you could purchase souvenirs, gifts, homemade fudge, salted nuts, sandwiches and assorted teas. All of this was available in an elegant seaside setting of guaranteed quality, especially of afternoon tea.

CLARA AND JOHN'S TEA ROOM, FREEPORT (1950–PRESENT)

This tea room started its life in Yarmouth as a small space run by John and Clara Hilton. In the 1950s, it was moved to Freeport on Route 1 and was open seasonally from June through October. During the season, the Hiltons worked sixteen to eighteen hours a day, six days a week! They ran the tea room for seventeen years before retiring. They obviously knew their business, as the tea room was widely known for its food, especially its lobster luncheons and homemade pies.

This tea room has been in the same location since that advantageous move in the 1950s to Freeport and has been in the café business from then to the present day, drawing a loyal customer base of locals and tourists and operating under the name the Freeport Café.

WHILE DINING IN THESE tea rooms, you would have enjoyed a sampling of a delicious dessert known as Mother's Ginger Tea Cakes found in nearly all tea rooms in Maine.

Mother's Ginger Tea Cakes

½ cup softened butter
1 cup sugar
2 eggs
⅔ cup dark molasses
1 cup rich (whole) milk
4 cups sifted flour
1 teaspoon salt

2 teaspoons powdered ginger
1 teaspoon cinnamon
1 teaspoon powdered cloves
1 teaspoon baking soda

Cream butter and sugar. Add eggs, molasses and milk and stir well together. Mix all ingredients and stir into creamed mixture. Drop by half-teaspoons on greased cookie pans about an inch apart and bake in preheated 400-degree oven for about 8 minutes (do not overbake).

When done, let stand a minute on cookie pans, then remove to cake racks to cool completely. Frost with an icing made of heavy cream and powdered sugar mixed to spreading consistency. When frosting has hardened, pack in a covered tin box with wax paper between layers of cookies.

American cities, including Portland, began building hotels with in-house tea rooms to accommodate all of the travelers visiting their great cities. Some of these tea rooms continued with the Colonial Revival décor, but just as the times were evolving, so was the décor of the tea rooms. People now considered the Victorian era as the height of refinement and elegance. So, the Victorian style became the guideline for decorating tea rooms. Flowers, lace, sparkling crystal, fine china, tables set with linen cloths, dainty chairs and lots of lights and mirrors became the new look of tea rooms. To help the transformation, walls were now painted in pinks, creams, grays or pastels to provide the in-vogue open, light and airy atmosphere.

A newspaper review of a tea room in 1938 reported:

> *The puddings are light as a summer cloud and the finest type of home cooking prevails. No beer or intoxicating drinks are served. The silver layout was correct from the first and the china was selected from a dainty, tasteful pattern. The linens are all bright and crisp and no customer would ever be expected to wipe his fingers on a paper napkin at this fine tea room! A very fine place, indeed.*

Barbara Dean's Tea Room, Ogunquit. *Author collection.*

Barbara Dean's Tea Room, Ogunquit (1934)

Opening in 1934, this tea room was destined to become one of Ogunquit's most popular restaurants. The building was one of the first guest houses in Ogunquit and was run by William H. Perkins until 1910. In 1934, the new owners, Ada Lent, Virginia Dean and Barbara Dean Knapp, opened a tea room in addition to the guest house. The tea room was furnished with many pieces of period furniture, offering a cheerful atmosphere and a panoramic view of the ocean.

Situated on the Shore Road at the entrance to Marginal Way, it entertained many notable people among its patrons. It was well known for its huge flower gardens on the oceanside lawns, its beautiful views and its great home-cooked meals. A lot of recipes used were taken from other parts of the country and adapted to Maine cookery. The specialty was blueberry gingerbread. A lot of the recipes were included in the national cookbooks of the time. A very popular tea room for many years, it was converted to condominiums in 1986.

MOST OF THE GRAND hotels had tea rooms that were great marble-pillared places lit by colored glass skylights and numerous chandeliers. The room was filled with tables elegantly draped with linen tablecloths accompanied by delicate-looking unique chairs, flowers and a small candle on each table, plus a fine menu—all of which added to the room's pleasurable setting among large potted ferns. Tea at these places was a bit more expensive than at your average tea room. At a time when the average price of a cafeteria meal was fifteen cents, a cup of tea alone was listed as twenty-five cents on a 1910 menu from the Copley Plaza Hotel in Boston, while a cup of tea or a glass of iced tea was listed as ten cents at the Puritan Tea Room in Portland.

THE DANISH TEA ROOM AT THE EASTLAND HOTEL, PORTLAND (1927)

The Eastland Hotel in Portland, home of the Danish Tea Room, was built by Henry P. Rines in 1927. He and his wife, Adeline, were frequent travelers to Europe and the Middle East, and they wanted to replicate some of the designs they had seen in their travels in their newly built hotel in Portland. The lobby, some of the rooms, the restaurant and the tea room

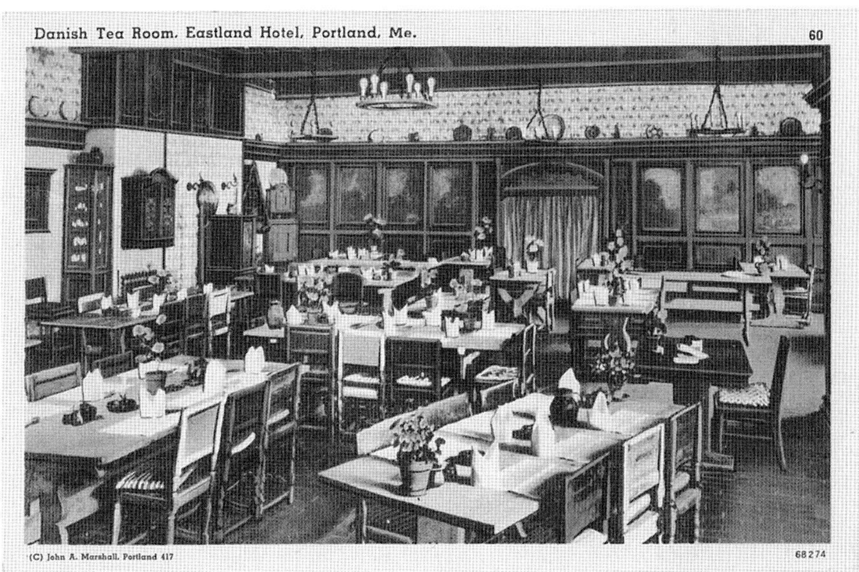

The Danish Tea Room at the Eastland Hotel, Portland. *Author collection.*

were all decorated with the décor of their favorite locations abroad in mind, including Denmark, Spain and Egypt.

The tea room was called *Skenkstuen*, which in Danish means "the place where patrons are served." It became more commonly known as the Danish Tea Room at the Eastland. The room is a substantial copy of Skenkstuen in Weis's Inn in the marketplace of Ribe, the capital of Denmark. The original tea room/tavern in Denmark is hundreds of years old.

Not only was the Eastland's tea room decorated to look Danish, but the Rineses also imported many of the decorative pieces used in the tea room directly from Ribe just for this room. All of this, including the crisp white linen, fresh flowers and great food, made for a very enjoyable and popular tea room for the city of Portland.

Soft, soothing music was also part of the hotel tea rooms. Most provided a dance floor with an orchestra to entice the trendy tea dance craze infecting the country during the early 1900s. An exotic and risqué dance originating from Argentina called the tango led to a nationwide enthusiasm for tango tea dances. The tango created so great a craze that everyone wanted to attend these tea dances. An interesting tidbit about the dances was that men were not allowed to attend the tea dance unless accompanied by women—quite a difference from earlier years! In addition to the tango, young people and college students loved going to tea dances to learn the newest dances of the day, like the bunny hug, the foxtrot, the turkey trot, the kangaroo dip and the grizzly bear. A lot of tea dances were also held benefiting charities and were well attended by young and old alike who helped to raise considerable monies for their causes. The introduction of the cocktail hour by the socially elite soon became the newest craze, however, and interest in tea dances languished and eventually ceased.

At the same time hotels were introducing tea rooms in their buildings, department stores were adding space for tea rooms to their floor plans. These in-house tea rooms offered shoppers a place to pause and refresh themselves in the midst of shopping. After being refreshed, it was the store owner's wish for the shoppers to continue shopping and buy even more! At this time, most shoppers wore hats and gloves, and they embraced the tea room movement as a sign of good manners and good taste, which delighted the store owners.

Puritan Tea Room, Portland (1920s–1960s)

The center of Portland's downtown shopping district offered many places to eat, and one of the most popular during its heyday was the Puritan Tea Room at 566 Congress Street. Its attractive storefront was a 1940s Art Deco design, and it offered an extensive menu.

The tea room offered sandwiches made to order the "Puritan Way," with mayonnaise or Russian dressing; entrées from steak to fish; soups, salads; omelets; refreshing drinks; and everything in between. Every Friday night offered a special menu. And they made all of their own pastries and candies. Dinner was served continuously from 11:00 a.m. to 11:00 p.m. This tea room operated from the 1920s to the 1960s and served many a fine meal throughout its many years of operation. For the people of Portland and especially for those shopping at the large department stores just steps away, it was the perfect place to get a hot cup of tea and a delicious meal.

Puritan Tea Room, Portland. *Author collection.*

THE VERY FIRST TEA room in a department store was in 1890 in the Marshall Field's department store in Chicago under the management of a man, not a woman. His name was Harry Selfridge, and with his assistant, Sarah Haring, he created a tea room of great and immediate success. It eventually seated three hundred and took up the entire floor of the store. At one time, this flagship store in Chicago boasted six tea rooms in one store.

After having established the success of the in-store tea room, Harry Selfridge cashed in his stock in the company for $1 million and promptly moved to London. He then proceeded to open a department store on Oxford Street based on American department stores. He replicated his Chicago tea rooms in the store. Selfridge was the first to offer in-store restrooms for his customers, which encouraged longer shopping hours. Within months of opening the tea room, Selfridges became *the* place for London ladies to take tea. Today, it is the second-largest department store in the United Kingdom, and you may still partake of refreshments at its in-house tea room.

Tea rooms in hotels and department stores at this time did not use cash registers. Most of the large tea rooms used little payment baskets that would zip back and forth over the heads of customers carrying customers' payments from the server to one central payment center usually one floor above the tea room. By the 1940s, these payment baskets were replaced by pneumatic tubes that rushed payment from floor to floor in half a minute or less. By the 1950s, these were replaced by cash registers.

Although department store tea rooms were basically the same in elegance and service, each one seemed to have its own special signature. For instance, Fredrik's and Nelson's Tea Room of Seattle held fashion shows every Wednesday during fashion season and twice a year featured a special showing of Paris dress originals. Gimbel's of New York allowed the filming of the movie *Miracle on 34th Street* to be done in its tea room and store, and this was always featured in its Christmas advertising. Filene's of Boston created the concept of the automatic bargain basement method of pricing, with reductions every week for thirty days, after which the items were donated to charity. Filene's well-attended tea room on the top floor was also the scene of an annual children's tea party, and during the 1920s, tea dancing was held there every week and proved very popular.

In the 1940s and 1950s, Maine department store customers began moving to the suburbs and doing most of their shopping there, as was happening nationwide. Department stores followed their customers to the suburbs, building small branch stores, which eventually led to the demise of patronage of most of the large department store tea rooms.

During the World War II years, the tea movement started its decline, with the tea rooms themselves all but vanishing, even in Maine. The slower pace of the tea room was being replaced by fast-food diners, drive-in restaurants and a much faster way of life.

From the 1960s to the 1990s, a pot of tea was mostly made from teabags, which in no way resembled the superior quality and taste of a cup of tea from earlier times that had been properly brewed and made from loose-leaf tea. The proliferation of the teabag removed the romance from the ritual of having tea while also changing the taste and quality of the tea itself. At that time, tea became a beverage that was enjoyed mostly at home or at a quick lunch out, and it was primarily being served as iced tea.

Today, tea and tea rooms are making a huge comeback. New students of the proper method of brewing teas along with their growing knowledge of the many, many different kinds of teas available are causing a new tea revolution. Health benefits are being discovered in teas, skin products are being produced from tea extracts and chefs are showing an interest in tea as a culinary ingredient. Afternoon teas are making appearances and becoming very popular again because of the many tea offerings available today, such as green teas, white teas and an extensive variety of black teas, all served hot or cold. The tea experience in Maine has developed into a strong following for the revival of tea, including its social aspect.

The phenomenal growth of specialty teas, tea table wares, tea companies, tea rooms, tea bars, tea classes, books and magazines and websites is evidence of the increasing interest today in teas and new tea experiences.

As a representative of women's culture and as a spokeswoman for a vital part of America's social history, tea rooms and their owners added a great deal to our way of life that continues today. A large contribution to this way of life was the role Maine women played in the tea movement of the twentieth century while establishing those pleasurable, elegant rooms for everyone's enjoyment.

Tea rooms established:

- The hiring of college girls as waitresses.
- The replacing of male maître d's with female hostesses.
- The acknowledgement that women could succeed in business.
- The realization that women and families constituted a solid customer base.

- The use of colorful restaurant names to replace common family names.
- That money could be made in the food business without serving alcohol.
- That people eating out loved home-cooked meals if served attractively and inexpensively.
- That popular outdoor dining was here to stay.
- An outlet for goods made from the arts and crafts movement.
- That restaurant interiors should be restyled to showcase atmosphere, elegance and relaxation.
- The use of candles and flowers as a permanent tabletop décor in restaurants.

Enjoying a proper soothing cup of tea today in the midst of our fast-paced world brings as much pleasure as it did when visiting the lovely tea rooms of yesterday for a cup of tea. The partaking of tea and the establishment of the tea room is considered to be a great part of America's social history, and its worth is reflected in the continuing interest in early tea rooms, the women who ran them and the great revival of the world of tea in today's world.

As Henry James once said, "There are few hours more agreeable than the hour dedicated to the ceremony known as afternoon tea."

BIBLIOGRAPHY AND LINKS

Attebery, Todd. "Daily Life of the American Colonies: The Role of the Tavern in Society." www.gothichorrorstories.com/the-history-trekker/daily-life-of-the-american-colonies-the-role-of-the-tavern-in-society.

Campbell, Mary Mason. *The New England Butt'ry Self Almanac*. Brattleboro, VT: Stephen Green Press, 1970.

Earle, Alice Morse. *Home Life in Colonial Days*. Williamstown, MA: Corner House Publishers, 1989.

Geake, Robert A. *Historic Taverns of Rhode Island*. Charleston, SC: The History Press, 2012.

The Henry Ford. "1891 Abbot Downing Concord Coach." www.thehenryford.org/collections-and-research/digital-collections/artifact/237451.

A History of Maine Roads 1600–1970. Augusta, ME: State Highway Commission, 1970.

Jones, Herbert G. *The King's Highway from Portland to Kittery*. Freeport, ME: Bond Wheelwright Co., 1953.

Little, Nina Fletcher. *Neat & Tidy*. Lebanon, NH: University Press of New England, 2001.

McRae, Angela Webster. *Dainty Dining*. Newnan, GA: self-published, 2011.

Oliver, Sandra. *Saltwater Foodways*. Mystic, CT: Mystic Seaport Museum, 1995.

Pettigrew, Jane, and Bruce Richardson. *A Social History of Tea*. Danville, KY: Benjamin Press, 2016.

Powell, Lyman P. *Historic Towns of New England.* New York: G.P. Putnam's Sons, 1898.

Sprague, Laura Fecych. *Agreeable Situations: Society, Commerce, and Art in Southern Maine, 1780–1830.* Kennebunk, ME: Brick Store Museum, 1987.

Standage, Tom. *A History of the World in 6 Glasses.* New York: Walker Publishing Company, 2005.

Struzinski, Steven. "The Tavern in Colonial America." *Gettysburg Historical Journal* 1, no. 7 (2002).

Wheeler, George A., and Henry W. Wheeler. *History of Brunswick, Topsham, and Harpswell.* Part II, chapter 8, "Taverns and Public Halls, Newspapers, etc." Boston: A. Mudge Printers & Sons, 1878.

Whitaker, Jan. *Tea at the Blue Lantern.* New York: St. Martin's Press, 2002.

INDEX

C

D

V

W

Y

ABOUT THE AUTHORS

Courtesy of Peter Goranites.

Kathy is a retired librarian whose deep love of books, history and antique quilts has led her to a second career as a quilt historian, educator, and lecturer. Her extensive vintage antique quilt collection allows her to enhance the different periods of America's history for her audiences and give them a closer, more hands-on approach to learning about various events in our nation's history, such as the story of tea and tea rooms during the years of the women's suffrage movement. She has been featured in several magazines and the featured speaker for a vast number of historical societies and women's groups from Maine to Colorado. Presenting a bit of history from a woman's perspective in this, her first book, reflects her many years of collecting stories of historical interest.

Bill Kenny, a former career U.S. Air Force logistics war planner, joint special operations commander, intelligence officer and Gulf War veteran and retired adjunct university professor where he taught international economics, public affairs, organizational leadership, and other courses at both the undergraduate and graduate levels, has always had a keen interest in history, especially Maine history. This is his second book; his first book released by The History Press in June 2020, titled *A History of Maine Railroads*, is a great success. Bill has traveled across the state and via Zoom to talk about this important time in Maine's history.

You can visit their website at www.historymaine.com.